Kay Morgan has no doubt that 'Souls in Jeopardy' has been written not by her but through her. She was given a message for mankind, an answer to the universal question, Why? In a straightforward, no nonsense manner, the book shows us how we can lead happier, more fulfilled lives. How to cope with fear, how to make seemingly impossible decisions, how we should bring up our children. In short, how to make the most of our world, the most of our lives.

Kay Morgan has deeply held religious beliefs but this book in no way preaches. Everyone who reads this book will feel that it has been written specially for them, will want immediately to follow the advice that Kay Morgan received, and start moving towards a better life and a better world.

'Souls in Jeopardy' is a book to give the world hope.

Kay Morgan trained as a beauty therapist and attended three world beauty congresses. She decided to become a remedial camouflage consultant in order to help individuals conceal disfigurements. This work was carried out in a specialist skin hospital, a burns and plastic surgery unit, and also privately.

Her first husband was a doctor, who died young; her son is also a doctor. Kay Morgan married again, and the recent loss of her third husband after less than three years of supremely happy marriage, has been a poignant experience of the pain and grief that are unavoidable challenges of human experience.

This book was written in the Cotswolds where she was living with her second husband.

To, Dear Hilda.
To be read in your quieter more peaceful moments after moving in to your new home.
From
 Morveyne 18·11·2000.

Best Wishes
Kay Morgan.

SOULS IN JEOPARDY

Kay Morgan

Temple House Books
Sussex, England

Temple House Books
is an imprint of
The Book Guild Ltd

This book is sold subject to the condition that it shall not, by way of trade or otherwise, be lent, re-sold, hired out, photocopied or held in any retrieval system or otherwise circulated without the publisher's prior consent in any form of binding or cover other than that in which this is published and without a similar condition including this condition being imposed on the subsequent purchaser.

The Book Guild Ltd.
25 High Street,
Lewes, Sussex

First published 1995
© Kay Morgan 1995
Set in Baskerville
Typesetting by Southern Reproductions (Sussex)
Crowborough, Sussex
Printed in Great Britain by
Antony Rowe Ltd.
Chippenham, Wiltshire

A catalogue record for this book is
available from the British Library

ISBN 0 86332 992 6

CONTENTS

Preface   9

Prelude   11
   The Morning After the Night Before — Fundamental Issues

Words of Truth   14
   The Question Why?' — Why Are You Afraid of Me? — The Way Back — Sin — Why Has the World Come to This?

Environment   21
   Litter — *Men Have Forgotten God* by Alexander Solzhenitsyn

Philosophy of Life   27
   To the Question — 'What Shall I Do?' — Freedom

Children   33
   Schools — Punishment — Child Abuse — Help for the Abusers — Divorce — Marriage — Families

Animals   45

Aspects of Life 46
> Alcoholism — Drugs — Morality — Self Discipline — Forgiving — Happiness — Diamonds — Caring — Envy — Jealousy — The Greener Grass — Relationships — Forcing Personality on Another — Assurance — Health — Feeling Down — Dishonesty — Despair — Suicide — Apathy — Killing - Murder - Wars — Tragedy — Being Impulsive — Boredom — Fanaticism — Rejection — Pity — Be Constructive — Existence

Love 90
> Love and Forgiving — Love, Peace, Happiness — Paul's Message to the Corinthians *(I Cor. 13)*

On Affairs of Mankind 94
> Actions and Influences of Thought — I'll do it 'My Way' — Fears — Confidence — Prayer — Beauty — Age — Retirement — Human Life

Conclusions 109
> Sermon on the Mount *(Matthew 5)* — Why Now?

Reflections 111
> Hope — Silence — Peace of Mind — Future

ACKNOWLEDGEMENTS

I should like to acknowledge the following authors and their works.

Men Have Forgotten God by Alexander Solzhenitsyn (with his personal very kind permission.)
Les Miserables by Victor Hugo
In Tune With The Infinite by Ralph Waldo Trine
Ulysses by Alfred Lord Tennyson

I wish to dedicate this book to my husband, David, who died so tragically before it was published, and to my son, Richard, who has been a great inspiration to me from the beginning.

Freedom

Since I wrote this book, wonderful things have taken place.

Freedom, which every individual throughout the world longs for, is now taking place in many countries.

The world's prayers and hopes are being answered.

PREFACE

This book has been written exactly as I have stated. It was definitely no dream but a definite instruction from 'The Highest Power', a direction for this generation – and future generations.

It is a guide to help people of the world, a philosophy of life, to know, without doubt, that life is eternal, and we must begin to live life NOW. to go forward, in the right way, not muddling through 'as if it all comes to an end anyway'. *It does not.*

It is a book for all people to understand, and with all hope, to benefit.

A Message
A message for everyday, ordinary men, women and children of all races and creeds.

A Message of Hope
A message from Divine Power, to this generation, a generation which finds itself in turmoil inherited from past generations – not all of its own making.

A Book for Understanding and Progress for All Mankind
The messages I received are sincere, unsophisticated and able to be used by all members of society throughout the world. There is absolutely nothing complicated.

PRELUDE

This book has been written because of an extraordinary experience

In the Beginning

I awoke in the night and was given a message that I was to write a book – that a book would be written through me with a message for the present generation, for all people, giving an answer to the question, 'Why?'

It is not a religious book but a practical book, guided by the 'Highest Authority'.

It is a book on human life. However, one cannot write on life and leave out our spiritual existence – the higher part of our lives, in reality, the real us – without quoting from fundamental beliefs and reality itself. In this respect one cannot leave out God, sometimes quoted as Deity.

'You must write a book. It will be dictated to you. It must be written to be read and accepted by all peoples, all colours and all nations, in order to help them to realise that life is eternal.'

'You have a year's probationary period – it must be published at the end of this time.'

'The name of the book is to be *Souls in Jeopardy*.'

This message came to me in the night. I awoke to feel a

'presence' in my room like a warm, misty glow. I was not at all frightened. A beautiful 'voice' spoke to me. It was also a feeling of 'knowing'. I knew exactly what was being said, absolutely clearly.

The Morning After the Night Before

I awoke on this beautiful October morning. It was cold, but the sky was blue, the fields green, covered deeply in early morning dew.

The room was warm and very light, with the sun rising and glistening on the dew like diamonds.

In this moment of truth, I knew that my life had completely changed. I was being led into a world as yet unknown. It was as if God was opening His arms and enfolding me, in peace, happiness and ecstasy. I knew I was to have no resistance to this 'New World' that I was being taken into.

I knew that I was being brought out of the shadows, into the light of day.

I knew I was touched by the hand of God.

The Voice told me that I was to write a book – that in reality it was to be written through me, to the peoples of this world, to tell them the Truth of Life – before they destroy the universe.

The world has got itself into such a mess, and it doesn't seem able to get itself out of it.

There is so much devastation, uncaring and unhappiness, and no one seems able to find the right answers.

The world was given to us by God, to look after and enjoy. We are to learn lessons here, before we go on to higher dimensions.

What an appalling mess we humans have made and

are making of this part of our existence.

What is rather difficult to understand, is why the generations of the world have come to such conclusions about life, death etc., instead of truth and reality of existence, which Christ tried to teach us.

Why do we not believe the Truth?

*

This is not a religious book as such. It is a book of messages, but as they are messages from the Highest Power, religion naturally plays a part in it.

If you are not at all religious, do not be put off. Read on, there are many messages which I am sure you will find helpful in this everyday world.

*

God is Spirit. There is no sex in Spirit. 'Men' means both sexes – men and women.

*

Fundamental Issues

What are the fundamental issues in life? The fundamental issues are:
1. A belief in God.
2. A belief in ourselves and other human beings.
3. A belief in an after life and life eternal.
4. To love and do good to all.
5. To do unto others as you wish done unto you.

WORDS OF TRUTH

The Question 'Why?'

Everyone the world over is asking the question: Why?

>Why are we here?
>Why the appalling tragedies?
>Why?
>Why?
>Why?

Who can answer this vital question? Many have tried.

No one has adequately been able to give a realistic answer.

Why should I be able to? I cannot of myself. The answers which I give have been given to me.

No human can give the answers. They have to come from a 'Higher Source'.

How does one know that the answers are from a 'Higher Source'? By intuition.

We are here to learn lessons in living. Because the answers are so simple, people doubt their authenticity. They prefer long drawn out explanations, which theologians try to give, and people doubt these – quite rightly!

However, if they will just give a little time and thought to the simple explanations, I believe they will understand.

People will ask: if it is true, why are we being told this now? Why haven't we been told before?

The answer comes that we are now a more advanced generation who can more easily assimilate what is being told us.

Because of the quite extraordinary things which are taking place, the 'Truth of Existence' will not be quite so 'out of this world' for us to understand.

*

We need a 'This Day' religion.

For true worship, only God and the human soul are necessary. It does not depend on times, seasons, or occasions. Anywhere and at any time, God and man can meet.

All is Law and all is cause and effect. As we sow, so shall we also reap, not only here in this life but in all lives.

Everything is for use but all must be wisely used in order to be fully enjoyed by everyone.

People are born with eternity in their hearts and they cannot escape the desire for meaning, which only eternal life can bring.

It is quite usual for people to ridicule what they do not understand.

*

The object of this book is to help all peoples of any nationality, colour, religion, age or sex, and to injure no one but to bless all mankind.

The pressures of life today – on all people – are so great

that many need help but don't know where to turn.

People may ask, why are we here? What is the purpose of life?

The answer must come surely from a 'Higher Power' than we mortals can express.

There must be an answer, but it must come from a Higher Source.

One may ask, why do we have children? Obviously because most individuals, inhabitants of this earth, wish to have children. Why then, if there is a God, should we not consider that God wanted children, and that is why He created them 'in His image and likeness' – spiritually.

People would say, what do you mean, spiritually? I am not spiritual, I am material. I have a material body and I live in a material world. I need doctors to keep me going. I need food to eat, and water (or alcohol!) to drink, otherwise I perish. There is nothing spiritual about me or anyone else.

Yes, we are living in a material world and so, while we are here, we need material bodies, but have you never had the feeling that there is *more* to you than something called 'body'?

Where does love come from? This is not a material substance. Where do feelings come from? They are not a material substance. Intelligence, fear, happiness, sincerity, appreciation and many, many other features cannot be called 'matter'.

Surely there is more to us than meets the eye. Somewhere are our real, spiritual selves.

Love cannot be removed by the surgeon! Neither can good or bad feelings, even hate. So where do they come from and where, if anywhere, do they go? In other words, what are we really?

One may say: how do we know that we go on from

here? No one has been back to tell us.

This is where so many people make mistakes. Because they have not had the experience of people coming back spiritually after death, they don't believe anyone who says that they have had the experience.

There are a great many 'ordinary' people who have experienced messages from beyond the grave. They are people of all nationalities. Unfortunately, unless they contact people who have had similar experiences, they are very rarely believed. They are afraid to tell most people because they will be ridiculed, laughed at and told they must be 'odd', until they begin to believe so themselves! It is a great pity that this happens, if these people were believed it could give the world an entirely new and different slant on life. It could answer many questions which go unanswered in what *seems* to be an entirely material world.

People may say, what does all this matter? It doesn't – or does it?

Many thousands of people throughout the world have 'died' during operations, accidents, illnesses etc. but have returned to this life. In other words, their spirits left their bodies but returned. They give testimonies about their experiences and say what wonderful experiences they were. Many didn't want to return to this life. They found the passing on to the next dimension and a glimpse of this marvellous, but for one reason or another, they returned. This has even happened to children.

I will not go into details of their experiences in this book, but there are many books on this subject if you wish to read about them.

*

The words that I write are being dictated to me; they are not something that has come from within myself but from outside this universe.

The people of this universe have reached a stage when they seem unable to draw back from destruction. They seem unable to help themselves any more – to put their lives into 'reverse gear'. There is a cry from the heart of the world for help, and a desire for a complete turnabout.

God knows this and is now ready to answer this call worldwide.

Within the depths of humanity there is a deep desire for love, goodness, happiness; the exact opposite to what is happening in the universe.

Good can always overcome evil. This is the centre and circumference of existence.

Why do we exist at all? Many people, probably most, ask themselves this, quite frequently. Because God wanted His universe to be inhabited by His children. So He gave them eternal life. Like all children, we have our lessons to learn, before progressing into higher spheres of existence. Like so many of our own children, we have made a real mess of our lives here – and of other people's, to the extent of being in danger of eliminating the planet.

This planet is a small part of our existence, somewhere for us to learn some lessons – what a mess we have made! There are so many people, or souls, who desire to be put on the right road again, before it is too late, that God is answering our call for help.

One may say, that's all very well, but how do we know all this? By *accepting the fact that there is a God,* that He cares for us limitlessly, that we must accept that we are spiritual – God made us in His own image and likeness – that life is eternal, and that there is no death, only a passing into the next stage of existence.

When these things are accepted, even by a small minority, great changes will take place and more and more people will come to realise and accept the truth of our eternal existence.

Why Are You Afraid of Me?

I am the eternal Life and circumference of the universe. *I own all. I am all.* 'I am that I am.'

I am *all* Love. You are my spiritual offspring. My children. *I love you all.*

Some have more to overcome than others, more lessons to learn.

Do Not Be Afraid. Fear destroys.

Nothing can destroy you, except yourselves, temporarily, until you realise that nothing can ever destroy you.

When you give Love, you receive Love.

The Way Back

The way back is there for all to take. It has to come through overcoming greed, selfishness etc.

The way back is by caring for yourself and others; by knowing and accepting that life *is* eternal, and by knowing that you have to pay the price for your sins here, or hereafter.

You do not have to pay for anyone else's sins, only your own. You are never rendered accountable for what others do, only for what you do yourselves, and reason is taken into account.

Sin

When a child is born, it has no sin but it has to learn lessons. That is why it is born into this world.

Unfortunately it picks up bad habits, or sin, along the way and these have to be eliminated. The child itself is a perfect spiritual idea of God. It is not a sinful being. The habits or sins have to be discarded here or hereafter, before we can go higher.

God gave us free choice. It is up to us to use this choice wisely.

Be not afraid, for *I* am the Lord thy God.

Why Has The World Come To This?

Much of the world's troubles are due to unmitigated greed and selfishness with no thought for others, or the world; or very little thought.

I gave you *All Choice, All Senses, All Dignity, All Abundance, Love* –

You have abused them.

ENVIRONMENT

This is a modern problem, brought on through thoughtless people and countries over many generations. Now our generation are confronted by a tremendous problem.

What is to be done about it? It is vital that all peoples and nations get together and begin to solve this problem. All nations must begin to realise that all countries will be affected if action is not taken *now*. We must be responsible for the future of our world – not destroy it.

What is to be done?

There must be a common world initiative and each country must help and advise the others, throughout the world.

Huge plants must be designed and built to recycle all disposable goods.

Research must be done to find the best materials for products, etc. which must be recycled.

No country or nation can tackle this problem on its own – it has to be a world environmental co-operation plan.

It must be decided what will be the best use for the recycled waste product, because it can become a product – whether for energy, new fertilisation of the land etc. A plan must be set up and put into action in this generation. It must not be left for future generations –

they will have their own problems to sort out.

Huge recycling-plants should be designed and built as soon as possible.

Litter

So many people do not seem to mind about making 'other places' a place to discard their litter. There should be more litter bins. These should be attractive, so as not to deface the surrounding area. They should be readily available in cities, towns, villages and the countryside. There could be a 'litter bin competition' to find the most useful and attractive ones. They should be regularly emptied, and people should use them.

The people of the world should endeavour to make all countries beautiful places and not just tidy ones. They would be much more pleasant places to live in.

Nothing should be wasted. The commodities of life have not been given to us to waste but to use wisely and with discretion. These include money, food, clothes, housing, other valuable resources and energy of all descriptions – even time! As the saying goes – 'Waste not, want not'.

God has provided the world with all that it needs – water, food, heat, light, everything.

Many wonderful things have been discovered and many more are waiting to be discovered.

It is the people who have caused wrong distribution. It is greed that causes wars, poverty, hunger, homelessness, and illness through malnutrition.

With correct distribution and help from the more advanced countries, the 'third world' and places of barren lands could be helped by proper use of reclaimed devastated land, so that eventually the people could become self-sufficient, in preference to handing out food and aid as the world is doing now.

Rain forests were planted by nature for nature's purposes.

It is wrong for human beings to destroy what was planted there for a purpose. Man knows this but is destroying it for greed.

The ones who are destroying nature's forests will not suffer themselves. They will no doubt gain tremendous financial benefits, but the devastation will be left for future generations to try to rectify.

Men Have Forgotten God
by Alexander Solzhenitsyn

When I started going to school in Rostov-on-Don – passing on my way a glittering sign of the League of Militant Atheists – school children taunted me for accompanying my mother to the last remaining church in town and tore the cross from around my neck. Later, I recall hearing a number of older people offer this explanation for the great disasters that had befallen Russia. 'Men have forgotten God; that's why all this has happened.'

Since then I have spent more than fifty years working on the history of the Russian Revolution; in the process I have read hundreds of books, collected hundreds of personal testimonies, and have already contributed eight volumes of my own towards the effort of clearing away the rubble left by the upheaval. But if I were asked today to formulate as concisely as possible the main cause of the ruinous Revolution that swallowed up some 60 million of our people, I could not put it more accurately than to repeat: 'Men have forgotten God; that's why all this has happened.' The failings of human consciousness, deprived of its divine dimension, have been a determining factor in all the major crimes of this century.

The Russian writer Dostoevsky warned that great events could come upon us and catch us intellectually unprepared. That is precisely what has happened. The present century is being sucked into the vortex of atheism and self-destruction. This plunge into the abyss has aspects that are dependent neither on political systems, nor on levels of economic cultural development, nor on national peculiarities.

It was Dostoevsky, once again, who said of the French

Revolution and its seething hatred of the church that 'revolution must necessarily begin with atheism.' That is absolutely true. But the world had never before known a godlessness as organized, militarized and tenaciously malevolent as that practised by Marxism.

Within the philosophical system of Marx and Lenin, and at the heart of their psychology, hatred of God was the principal driving force, militant atheism a central pivot. The degree to which the atheistic world longs to annihilate religion, the extent to which religion sticks in its throat, was demonstrated by the web of intrigue surrounding the attempt on the life of Pope John Paul II in 1981.

Yet in Russia, where churches have been levelled, where a triumphant atheism has rampaged uncontrolled for two-thirds of a century, where the clergy has been humiliated and people sent to labour camps for their faith, the Christian tradition still survives. There remain many millions of believers acutely and profoundly aware of God. It is here that we see the dawn of hope.

The West has yet to experience a Communist invasion and religion is free. But the West, too, is experiencing a drying up of religious consciousness. This gradual sapping of strength from within is a threat to faith that is perhaps even more dangerous than any attempt to assault religion violently from without.

Imperceptibly, through decades of gradual erosion, the meaning of life in the West has ceased to be seen as anything more lofty than the 'pursuit of happiness'. The concepts of good and evil have been ridiculed, banished from common use. They have been replaced by political or class considerations of short-lived value.

It has become embarrassing to appeal to eternal concepts, embarrassing to state that evil makes its home in the individual human heart before it enters a political system. Western societies are losing more and more of their religious essence as they thoughtlessly yield up their younger generation to atheism.

Atheist teachers in the West are bringing up a younger generation in a spirit of hatred of their own society. This eager fanning of the flames of hatred is becoming the mark of today's free world. Indeed, the broader the personal freedoms are, the higher the level of prosperity or even of abundance – the more vehement, paradoxically, does this blind hatred become. The West thus demonstrates that human salvation can be found neither in the profusion of material goods nor in merely making money.

With global events looming over us like mountains, it may seem incongruous to recall that the primary key to our being or non-being resides in each individual human heart, in the heart's preference for specific good or evil. Yet this is the most reliable key we have. The social theories that promised so much have demonstrated their bankruptcy, leaving us at a dead end.

All attempts to find a way out of the plight of today's world are fruitless unless we redirect our consciousness, in repentance, to the Creator of all. Life consists not in the pursuit of material success but in the quest for worthy spiritual growth. Our entire earthly existence is but a transitional stage in the movement to something higher, one rung of the ladder. Material laws alone do not explain life or give it direction.

To the ill-considered hopes of the last two centuries we can propose only a determined quest for the warm hand of God, which we have so rashly and self-confidently spurned. Only in this way can our eyes be opened to the errors of this unfortunate twentieth century and our hands be directed to setting them right.

A PHILOSOPHY OF LIFE

Once more, I wish to say that I have not written this book, it has been written through me. This is the reason I believe that what I am writing is true. Otherwise, why should the messages be forthcoming?

What happens in this life is a plus or minus for our next existence.

If we go on from this existence into the next one it surely means that we have arrived in this existence from a previous life or lives. Is this the reason why so many lives differ; why some have so much and other virtually nothing? Does how we have behaved in our previous life, or lives, determine our place in this life? It would seem so. Also many people feel they have met someone before, when in actual fact they have never met before in this life. The chances are that they have been close to them in previous existences.

I believe that God is giving us this message for us to think very clearly about it.

> *In the beginning God created the heaven, and the earth ... And God said, Let us make man in our image, after our likeness ... So God created man in His own image, in the image of God created He him. Male and female created He them ... And God saw everything that He had made, and, behold, it was very good.*
> *(Genesis 1:1, 26,27,31)*

And God made man spiritual, in 'His image and likeness'.

Did He? Do you believe it? How do we know?

What proof have we? In our material world, we doubt almost everything which does not conform to our 'apparent' materialistic world.

The proof surely is that these messages are being given to us.

There is no (racial) colour in Spirit, therefore as we are all spiritual in reality, no one is any different from anyone else, whatever the colour of their human bodies.

Human experiences are a learning and proving ground.

Prayer puts us *in tune* with a deep spiritual reality that harmoniously corrects human problems.

Spiritual reality is free to all. It satisfies us. It makes us whole. It gives us a solid reason for living.

They are all plain to him that understandeth, and right to them that find knowledge. (Proverbs 8:9)

The world has lost its way. Why? There are many reasons, but selfishness, greed and the desire of so many humans who wish to be the 'Big I Am', without caring what unhappiness or damage etc. they do others, are some. All they care about is 'self'. Often they seem to lack the ability to have any feeling for others – even those closest to them, so obviously they will not care what they do to the rest of mankind.

Unfortunately, these types of people seem to forge ahead, pushing their way forward, over the heads of nicer, more considerate people. They take the best of everything they can lay their hands on, far more than their needs, so depriving others of their share of life.

These people are usually atheists or agnostics – they

couldn't behave the way they do if they had any belief in a Higher Power. So they do not care who they trample underfoot.

Sometimes these people are brought to their senses by illness, bereavement or even by being over-ruled by others who are even worse than they are, and they find themselves being destroyed by others' greed.

This present existence is a stepping stone along life's highway.

God made us His children. He made us perfect (spiritually), but like our own 'perfect' children, we have to grow and learn many lessons to mature. We stumble along the way, we fall over.

We are all completely individual, in every way. We are always helped, when we seek it, in the right way. As has been said, 'God helps those who help themselves.' They ask and receive not, because they ask amiss.

When man eventually faces the reality that there is no death, that life continues on another plane of existence, he will advance more radically towards life as it really exists.

Life can be like a dark tunnel, going through it and coming out on the other side.

There is a Supreme Spiritual Being, a God, who cares, who forgives the most outrageous failings. There are also people in this sphere of life who are willing and able to help, even the most seemingly hopeless cases, on to a new start in life. Everyone can be guided to a new beginning and helped to make a forward stride into a happy, fulfilling future that leads eventually through the 'Open Door', into the next existence.

God can use people in many different ways to help others to pick up the pieces of their lives and to give them some hope, confidence and understanding. It is possible to realise that whatever has gone wrong, can be put right.

One just has to be repentant, really want to be helped, and believe, and the help is there for them.

Life is eternal. Let us start to live right now in this sphere of our present existence. It will be a tremendous step forward when we eventually enter the next 'sphere'.

In his novel *Les Miserables*, Victor Hugo tells of the terrible plight of the many poor and homeless people of France in the early 1800s, and of the ongoing struggle for freedom, equality and dignity.

At one point Hugo writes:

> *Will the future ever arrive? . . . Should we continue to look upwards? Is the light we can see in the sky one of those which will presently be extinguished? The idea is terrifying to behold, lost as in the depth, small isolated, a pin-point brilliant but threatened on all sides by the dark forces that surmount it. Nevertheless, no more in danger than a star in the jaws of the clouds.*

For many, the future seems uncertain of changing and often hopeless at times, holding little promise. But one can look through the haze and darkness and see a light still shining.

People who have courage feel within themselves that even if the light seems almost extinguished by sadness and misery, the darkness cannot really overwhelm the light. The light is actually like a star which has been in 'the jaws of the clouds', but the clouds will finally disappear, blown away by the wind. The star will then be shining again in all its brilliance.

Most people are not as miserable or as hopeless as Victor Hugo describes in *Les Miserables*. Times have fortunately changed. However, there are people who do feel pretty hopeless from time to time. Usually one of the worst things one can say to these people is, 'Pull yourselves together' if they are in deep distress. They must get outside help. People who are told this can get terribly angry with the feeling that, 'No one understands me.'

Please, never say 'pull yourself together', unless it is a very slight case of, 'I just feel fed up.'

Life is not supposed to be easy: enjoyable – yes, in our present existence. We are here to learn lessons, sometimes the hard way, but the sooner we realise this, the sooner we can turn some of the lessons into helpful and happy steps forward.

*

To the Question 'What Shall I Do?'

When in doubt, when you have to make an important decision, or a very important decision – when you do not know what to do in the circumstances about a difficult problem – you ask what shall I do, what is the right decision to make?

The correct question to ask yourself is , *'What is the right thing to do in the circumstances?'* When you do this, and act on this to the very best of your ability, this is the correct answer. No one can do more. It doesn't matter what it is. If it does not turn out to be right, you will be guided to take the right action. Make sure your motives are right.

If you pray, you will be guided to make the right decision.

Freedom

Freedom is a stirring word. It probably serves as a rallying cry for more people and causes throughout the world than any other.

We instinctively want freedom for ourselves and for everyone. We want freedom from outward tyranny, from inward self-doubt, from want of every description and from whatever would suppress human fulfilment.

Many people feel locked into the limits and patterns of their lives. For some it is egotism or self love, and that holds them hostage.

To be truly free, we obviously need to have power over what would most limit our freedom.

The New Testament says, 'Where the Spirit of the Lord is, there is liberty.'

We are much more likely to find liberty within ourselves if we have honesty, goodness, affection, moral courage, and are upright, if we are people who are doing our best in life in whatever position we may find ourselves.

According to the Law of Life, we are 'born free', and should remain so for the rest of our lives. Unfortunately, this is very rarely so. Different things happen to different people during their lives, and they lose their sense of freedom.

CHILDREN

We do not have to learn a lot of psychological theory and teach it to our children. If we love our children as affectionately as possible and with understanding, they will do the rest. If we accept ourselves and them, they will learn to accept themselves and others.

In time, the day may come when each unworried baby grows up to be what one modern parent stated was his aim for his child: 'A newer kind of human being; an aware person, with love and without fears. An adequate, sound individual, able to live anywhere in the world, loving life, always.'

Children who are brought up in normal relaxed homes, where parents enjoy each other and the children, will tend to be like those little toys with lead in the bottom. No matter who throws them or where, they will land upright.

Many people wonder if babies have worries. They certainly do, especially about losing their parents. Babies need love as plants need the sun, in order to grow upright, strong and able to cope with life's storms in later life. It is better, of course, for children to get love direct from their parents, but if for some reason this cannot be so, they will benefit by receiving it from someone else: grandparent, nurse, sister, brother or friend and guardians.

The feeling that we are loved is wonderful, but for children it is essential. A child who is loved feels worthy of being loved. If a child is not loved it feels that no one cares, apparently they are not worthy of being loved and what happens to them doesn't matter. They are not important to anyone and they do not have the same incentive as the loved ones to make all kinds of efforts.

It is a well-known psychological fact that one who has been loved as a child can love and think well of himself, or herself, as an adult. This is particularly true when applied to persons who are ugly or deformed. If they were truly loved in their growing years, they stand a healthy chance as adults of carrying their handicap with dignity and self-respect and living happy lives, enjoying deep relationships and achieving their potential.

I personally know of a case where a young person had an extremely deformed mouth. Surgery could not help. It was 'camouflaged' by someone very skilled in this work. However, it was still quite unsightly. I asked this person if it worried her very much. She said, 'Oh no, it doesn't worry me. I have a good job, travel quite a lot and meet lots of people.' It must have taken great courage to be able to do this. However, she said that her mother was always cheerful throughout her childhood and never seemed worried about her daughter's deformity. I am quite sure that her mother's attitude, whatever she suffered silently, had been the root cause of this young person's ability to cope with her life so successfully.

This young lady also told me that she had been to Canada and, whilst there, she had to attend a Canadian hospital. The young doctor she saw looked at her and said, 'My, you have got a problem!' She told me that she considered that it was the doctor who had the problem, to speak to a patient in such a way!

Not giving children fears does NOT mean that you should not make them very aware of dangers. Of course you should do this to protect their lives. You must explain to them the dangers in a kind and loving way. If you explain to them thoroughly, in this way, they will remember and heed instructions.

Never have, or at least show that you have, a favourite child, however difficult this may be to overcome, or to hide. This must be done to prevent the child or children who are not the favourite one from growing up with at least a 'chip' on their shoulder, or much worse. Deep inferiority complexes, which can wreck their lives – and others', could be the result. Also, being the favourite one can have a bad effect, the child becoming superior, or even a bully.

Building children can be like building a house. The foundations must be solid and strong to weather any future storms of life, to overcome fear, malice and human will.

A life built on strong foundation will weather any storm.

Children are lent to us.

Children must be treated as individual people and not talked down to. However, they must be disciplined in the correct way.

Children are much more forgiving and resilient little creatures than most people give them credit for.

Always tell children the truth, however difficult it may be. They will understand much more than one may think. They will appreciate that you have told them the truth, and what is extremely important, they will know that they can trust you.

Many mothers, in rearing their children, load them down with fears and penalties and thereby plant seeds of disease and suffering. The majority of a mother's fears have no more foundation then the ghost stories which frighten children and disturb them mentally and physically. Many fears are of man-made origin and act disastrously on the health and well-being of the child.

'Helping Mum' probably gives as much pleasure to a child as a whole roomful of expensive toys.

It is much better for us to use our 'common sense' in bringing up children from birth onwards. Too much nonsense is written by people who don't have much idea on the needs of individual people and their offspring.

If you read books and articles on child care and bringing up children, take the best of what is written and reject the rest. Your own common sense will pay dividends.

Parents, guardians and all people who have contact with children must realise the impact that their 'innocent' remarks and conversations may have on the child concerned. One true case I will relate gives some insight into what can result from a parent's not thinking or realising the result of a 'threat'.

A girl of about nine years of age lived in a nice house, in a good environment and with loving parents. She was well brought up and was usually a well-behaved child. However, one day she was a bit rebellious against parental control – which was usually rather restricting. On this particular day, although the girl was not behaving as her mother thought she should, it was in fact the mother who was going through a difficult period and this was being directed against the child.

The mother told the girl that if she didn't behave herself, she would pray to be taken away from the child. The child adored her mother and the threat had such an impact on her that the child went almost hysterical, and begged and begged the mother not to do so. The mother no doubt completely forgot the episode, but not so the child. During the whole of her childhood and adolescence she lived in fear and dread of losing her mother. It almost completely marred any real happiness she could have had. When she went to stay with relatives, with her mother, a year or so later, the following episode shows the extent of her fears. They were staying with the mother's sister and sister's husband. Her uncle was a lawyer and they had no children of their own. He was very fond of his niece and she was used to staying with them from a very young child.

One evening, her mother and aunt went to the theatre, leaving the girl in bed and her uncle to babysit. However, the girl woke up and called for her mother. It had been decided to tell the child, if she asked, that her mother had gone to see some neighbours. Well, the girl suddenly felt that she may never see her mother again, that her mother had left her, and she started to cry. When her mother didn't return, the girl started to scream. She just couldn't stop. Her uncle became quite distraught and asked a neighbour to fetch her mother from the theatre. The girl kept on screaming until her mother returned. When she saw her mother come through her bedroom doorway, she immediately stopped crying, and said, 'Hello, Mummy'. Everyone thought what a naughty child she was, including her mother, who had had to leave the theatre. However, the child was not 'naughty' at all but terrified that her mother had left her and that she would never see her again. The sight of her mother returning to her made her feel secure again.

Never, never threaten a child with anything adverse – it can continue to haunt the child, even for life.

Mothers and fathers must train their children in love and understanding for others. Teach them to face difficulties – not to avoid them. Teach them that difficulties are part of life which they should overcome without undue reluctance and fear.

Teach them to obey you, so that they will obey the rules of life in happiness and understanding. Give them love, understanding and fairness, but be firm when necessary. If you say a definite NO! explain to them why you have said no, and if there should be a specific reason for this, do not alter your decision, or they will begin to think that they can always get their own way. This would not help them to face life in the future. However, you must explain to them why you have said no to them. They will learn to trust your decisions.

Children must have discipline as well as love. It makes them feel secure – that someone really cares for them.

Schools

Discipline in schools must be adhered to and respect for teachers must be upheld.

Surnames, not Christian names, for teachers make for more respect.

Teachers should behave themselves in a manner to gain respect.

A child must be encouraged to do things. They usually do not try, or continue to do things, without encouragement.

Punishment

Children should be punished for bad behaviour. Never threaten a child unless you intend to carry it through. Otherwise the child will know that he or she is able to do what they please, without punishment for wrongdoing, and will almost certainly progress to worse behaviour.

After warning them, if they persist, an appropriate punishment should be given.

Something they want at the time can be withheld until they realise that bad behaviour does not get them all they want.

It is important that children are not spoilt. We all want to give good things to our children, but they must learn that it is not possible to have everything we want when we want it. Sometimes we must do without, or wait for a period with patience.

Child Abuse

Child abuse is a horrific evil. Not only does it usually wreck the life of the child who is abused, but it is often passed down to future generations by the one who was originally abused. These children are often the victims of the people who were first abused. Fortunately these things are now coming to light and are more easily dealt with in this more enlightened age. However, there are of course reasons why the person who is the abuser does such a terrible crime. It cannot be just for personal gratification; it must run more deeply than that.

In this present age of 'I want, I get' attitude in so many and various aspects of life, it is not surprising that child abuse is so prevalent.

Help for the Abusers

It surely would be a much better idea to have a special place where abusers could be sent, rather than prison which cannot help or cure many of these people.

It would be practical to convert a large unused

building to be a type of 'prison hospital', where these people can be treated medically and in other ways, so that there is at least a chance for them to be able to become a part of the community once they are released. I do not mean to be lenient with them, but to help both them and their families, and also the overcrowded prison service. They could be made (in most cases) to realise the terrible devastation and suffering they are causing to the young victims. Video shows etc. could be presented to them, along with medical and psychiatric help, which would show the horror of the suffering of their victims and what could happen to future generations through their appalling behaviour.

Cases for this type of rehabilitation would obviously have to be sorted out. Prison would be right only in some cases. Medical and social help should be available for the judges. It would be impossible for a judge to 'sort out' the right cases.

We must stop the appalling, destructive behaviour before it gets more hold on the population of the world. We were not given our bodies and emotions to destroy but to use in rightful ways. These people are not always just wicked. They too need help and understanding.

Divorce

Children are usually torn apart by divorce. Parents often take little or no account of the children, who love both parents, and so the children are usually devastated whatever their age when their parents part.

This is rarely taken into account by parents, who are so wrapped up in their own domestic upheaval that the emotional well-being of the children is neglected.

Divorce is taken much too lightly by many people.

Some people think that by changing partners problems will melt away. This usually is not so, many take on more responsibility with a second family, also one does not usually alter and the same problems become even more difficult.

Many people, both men and women, have said that they have regretted a divorce. Do look before you leap.

Marriage

Marriage is the legal and moral provision for human beings whilst in this sphere of existence. Also there is no stability in marriage without chastity. Society would 'fall apart' without it.

The union of masculine and feminine qualities constitutes completeness. There are many difficulties and trials to be overcome.

A happy and contented marriage can be one of life's most wonderful experiences. However, an unhappy marriage can be one of life's most devastating experiences, not only for the unhappy couple but for all concerned.

Happy marriages do not just 'happen'. They have to be 'worked at', often very hard and sometimes for long periods of time, but this is more then well worthwhile.

No one should expect a happy marriage to 'just happen', as so many people seem to believe.

When people get married, often they seem to consider that 'that's that. Now I can relax.' By all means 'relax', but do not relax manners, hygiene and personal attractiveness, in many ways, including dress.

One should continue to think of one's husband or wife

as someone special, to show good manners to, to say 'thank you' to, for all things one says 'thank you' for before marriage.

If you are a woman, always endeavour to look your best, even in the morning! When your husband returns in the evening, greet him as if you are pleased to see him, and again, look your best. No doubt you will say, 'After all I have had to do all day, I don't feel my best!' You would have had plenty to do during the day before you were married, but if your boy-friend was going to take you out, or spend the evening with you, no doubt you would have done your best to look nice. Now you are married, I am sure your effort would be appreciated.

The men should also follow this form. I am sure the partner would appreciate this and feel the menfolk really care.

Kindness, generosity and love go a long way towards a harmonious marriage – which everyone seeks, but rarely seems to find these days.

Children pick up things very quickly from their parents and all these things would be appreciated by them. They would realise the good things and would eventually carry them forward into their own marriages.

Families

The idea of the mother staying at home and bringing up the family, as in the time of our grandparents, has almost faded out. Now, in many homes, both parents go out to work.

This leaves the children, in many cases, to their own devices, and can lead to trouble.

The mother, when she returns from work, is usually

tired but she still has her chores to do; which are usually many, including feeding hungry mouths. Shopping has to be done, often during the lunch breaks.

It is quite obvious that mother often thinks she cannot do much for her children and tells them to go and play outside or to watch the television.

The family is being brought up without the background of a full and happy family life, and often weekends are made up of the same sort of pattern, with the mother trying to catch up on her chores.

This sort of life not only deprives the children of a full and happy existence but deprives the parents also. They cannot enjoy a fulfilling family life.

What can be the answer to this existence? Something which could change the pattern and give a much happier and fulfilling life?

What could change things, would be help in many ways. If mothers have a part-time employment, this would give the mother a chance to 'get away from home', which so many desire, and also to earn money to help the family budget.

There could be another 'army' of mothers, teenagers and unmarried women, retired and widows, who could be properly trained. School curriculums should include a proper domestic training. These helpers could go to the houses and do many of the chores. Women with young babies could also do this work. It would get them out of their own environment and enable them to earn a little extra cash.

Would it not be possible to have some sort of public scheme, where many of the helpers could be paid, or partly paid, by the Council, and the rest from the person they have been working for?

There should be a definite school course for all children to learn how to cope with home and children, economics, catering and general relationship courses. These courses would be extremely helpful, when the children marry.

Young people are often thrown into life and marriage, many without any idea how to cope with these basic facts of life. It is definitely not something which comes naturally to most young people, it is almost always something which has to be learned.

Unfortunately, in so many cases, it is learned the hard way and perhaps it is the cause of unhappiness, hopelessness and the break-up of many marriages.

It is not possible for any mother to have a full-time job and to run a home and family successfully without help. It is physically impossible. It also destroys any 'quality of life' which should be enjoyed by herself and the family. The exceptions are people with money or well paid employment, who can employ others to help.

Drug usage and crime among young people, and even children, are often caused through a disintegrated family life.

ANIMALS

Animals are in this world in their own right and are not second-rate human beings.

Animals have their own fears and we human beings should recognise this and treat them with respect.

Why some human beings treat animals as if they have no feelings is beyond comprehension. It is not only cruel, it is wicked.

Not everyone loves or even likes animals, but everyone can be kind and considerate.

All ways and means should be used to the very best advantage to alleviate suffering, both mental and physical, when animals are taken to slaughter. The most modern methods should be used throughout the world.

Parents should teach their children to respect animals.

ASPECTS OF LIFE

Alcoholism

Alcoholism is one of the biggest scourges of mankind. It has been around for innumerable generations – long before the present drugs were ever thought of.

Many generations have had the lives of whole families ruined by alcoholism. Both men and women suffer from it, but it is more usual to be on the male side. It can overtake one at almost any age.

There is a big difference between the 'social drinker' and a true alcoholic. Many people can have a lot to drink, much more than is good for them, but never become alcoholics.

Most alcoholics cannot help themselves, they need professional help to enable them to overcome this 'disease'. To begin with, they must definitely want to give it up, otherwise everyone is wasting time trying to help. Many say they want to give up drinking and probably think so themselves and try to do so on their own. However, after a time they revert back to their old habits.

Everyone must have tremendous patience, especially the families of these people. The alcoholics themselves must have great determination to fight this scourge. They must realise the awful distress, pain and humiliation they are causing those nearest to them. If they really care and do not want to wreck the lives of those nearest to them, they will fight with all the determination they can muster, seek professional help and banish this awful mental, physical and soul-destroying 'curse'.

They *can* do this, with the right help, however long they have been alcoholics and whatever age they are. When they have won their battle, they will find a great personal 'freedom'.

Alcoholics Anonymous is an organisation especially for helping alcoholics. It has helped innumerable people over many years. If you are uncertain how to get in touch with them, ask your doctor, or find them in the telephone directory. When you have decided to go to them, you must continue, however hard it may be, to do exactly as you are told, until you come out of this dark tunnel into the glorious light of day. Do not feel humiliated or timid. Many famous people have conquered alcoholism in this way, and so can you.

If you wish to get help on a more medical basis (alcoholism is considered to be connected with one's physical make-up) do not feel ashamed to ask your doctor to recommend other help from medical people or others specialising in this work.

No one will look down on you for seeking help. They will all rejoice when they see the real 'you' emerging from the nightmare of alcoholism. Save yourself and your families. Do pray to God for His help.

'Social' drinking is in quite a different category. However, if taken to excess, it can also cause much misery to the families concerned. Like most things taken to excess, it ceases to be a pleasure and becomes quite unpleasant.

Apart from letting one's partner down by alcoholic behaviour, it can turn what started out as a pleasant evening, party etc. into something more like a nightmare.

Drinking and driving is not only extremely dangerous and stupid, but wicked. It is often other people on the road who suffer worst in an accident. Innocent people who were doing everything right often suffer the consequences of another's foolish behaviour.

Alcohol is quite an expense and for people who are not well off it can cause great hardship in families. Do realise this and drink reasonably and not excessively.

A great many people find happiness and pleasure in 'social' drinking and not 'excessive' drinking. Do be one of these.

Drugs

There are many and varied reasons why people of all ages begin to take drugs.

Many young people do it 'to see what it is like' and once taken they want more. Others take them for 'kicks'. They enjoy the feel of being 'high' on them and then become addicted.

Other users often start to take drugs because of their boring, everyday world of high pressure, or domestic unhappiness. The feeling of being 'high' on drugs becomes an addiction and unless addicts make a tremendous effort and get the right sort of help, their lives become hopeless and they often have an untimely death.

When drug takers have had a dose of a drug, they feel they can conquer the world. The euphoria is unbelievable. While it lasts, they feel wonderful – whatever their positions, wherever they are.

From a palace to a hovel, the effect is the same. The

length of time it lasts is according to the drug and dosage. However, in no way does it last long. Suddenly one can feel the withdrawal symptoms. It is like the life blood being drained from one. The recognition that you are not the person you believed you were whilst under the drug's influence is like a shock to the system. The withdrawal becomes more intense and whatever the position you were in, you begin to feel at 'rock bottom'. Sometimes it can be as bad as feeling like 'hitting hell'. The realisation of this terrible state and the mental knowledge that you are only 'you', as you were before you took the drugs, becomes too much for most of the 'takers'. Their hatred of themselves becomes so intense that they do not care that continuing to take the drug will destroy them. Their only desire is to get back into the euphoria which they have just left. The addict's tolerance to drugs quickly builds up; larger amounts are needed to give the feeling of euphoria, the more they take, the more they need. The need becomes so great that nothing, just nothing, will prevent them from getting more.

Stealing, even murder, does not count with some addicts. They only have one desire – to get back to the euphoria. No loyalty, love, pleading, begging, prison, nothing that anyone can say or do will change them. They just do not care who they destroy in this desire to return to the euphoria – where they think they rule the universe.

The ones who have a desire to return to normality are the drug addicts who have within themselves faith, love and a desire not to hurt themselves or others. A belief in life, God and a hope of eternity. A knowledge within themselves that life is to be lived on this planet and not abused with artificial drugs. Decency, a thought for others, a dislike of lies, stealing are abomination to them. In other words, they are decent human beings who know within themselves right from wrong and care about it.

In many cases these people have been brought up with a knowledge of religion, either in their houses or in their schools, where the morning sessions in school started with morning prayers. They usually have a warm and loving relationship with their parents or guardians.

They have a terrible struggle to overcome the drugs. More than can be put into words. However, the ones who are determined to return to normality and lead decent lives again eventually win through.

They need tremendous help from all concerned. If they lapse, they must not be rejected in any way. Rejection, even in the slightest, can send them back on drugs. In fact in some cases they will even 'test' the ones concerned by being quite horrible to them. This is obviously a tremendous trial to the ones trying to help, especially their loved ones.

It is like a mountain which must be climbed and conquered. When you reach the top of the mountain, the view beyond is glorious to behold – you have won a tremendous battle. The scars need healing but you know you have won, you know that from this moment your battle is over and from now on life is going to be wonderful. You can face any future battle in life with the knowledge that you are strong enough to cope with anything.

It may not work in many cases. Even those with a knowledge of religion from an early age will reject all.

It is a certain 'something' within the person which will accept the certainty of eternal life, a seed of belief that there is a God and that He really will help.

When they accept this 'feeling' and reach out to God, all 'heaven' is let loose to help them. It is as if forces come along and carry them with them, on to a higher plane, where they are able to fight their abuse with all the love, care and help imaginable. No holds barred – they are literally taken care of.

Some have a 'built in' knowledge and feeling which has nothing to do with upbringing, religion or family. It is an inner realisation that life is more than meets the eye, an inner message. There are people who will fight any battle and win through and they are usually prepared to help other people fight their battles. They are men and women that others cannot destroy, however hard they may try. They hold on as if holding the invisible hand of God. Help comes to them in an invisible way. When they begin to recognise this they receive more help, until they become complete beings and are able to go forward and help others.

The people selling drugs, the 'pushers', and especially the 'leaders' or 'barons', have death and destruction on their hands. Greed is their motive and they have no pity towards the innocent people they destroy. They will even turn children into addicts and the unborn children of addicts are completely helpless in this terrible human destruction.

The human misery is beyond measure.

All countries and people the world over must fight this terrible modern scourge with every possible means.

For example there are some people, the Mafia and even some so-called 'ordinary people', who have no faith in anything. Nothing on earth would deter them from their 'chosen profession', whatever it may be. They are utterly selfish. Even if Christ himself came and talked to them, they would continue in their way of life. They wouldn't listen or alter in any way. It would not make an atom of difference to them.

They will not allow anything to get in their way. All they care about are themselves, or what they can get out of this life and out of other people. The fact that they are capable of destroying other lives, and often do, never deters them for a moment.

Fundamentally, they are awful cowards. If anything is in danger of touching them, let alone hurting them, they will destroy it without a second thought before it has time to do much damage, whatever it may be. A human being, however close – wife, child, parent, friend, all will be sacrificed for their greed and desire for self-aggrandisement.

Many of these people seem to thrive in this world. They advance into big business, even professions.

From a human point of view they seem to have everything. Never envy this type of person.

It may sound rather smug to say they will get their deserts, but this is precisely what will happen, when they 'awake' in the next sphere, they will realise that they haven't died. The shock will be quite great for them, that there is no death, that they must face problems which they have just left.

How do people who are close to the 'outcasts of society' deal with them? They don't. They can't. However hard one tries, whatever method one uses, it is almost always of no avail. Nothing will change them at this point in 'time'. Whatever obligations one may feel, it is no use trying to reform them – only God can do this. It is better for everyone to leave these totally selfish well alone, to their own devices, whatever terrible mess thay make of their lives. In some cases the authorities will take over.

The only positive thing one can do is to try and help the people who have got themselves entangled with them. Those close to them or who have unfortunately met them and been taken in by them. These people need all the help and friendship they can get. Even professional help may be needed. Lawyers, doctors, counsellors etc. Do all you can to help these people – they are the worthwhile ones, but unfortunately vulnerable to sharp talk etc. Many may be completely ruined monetarily, mentally and physically.

Never ever give these 'outcasts of society' money, property or anything they ask or beg for, whatever method they use to pull the wool over your eyes. Do not be tricked by false promises of rich rewards, letting your greed allow you to be conned. The chances are they will swindle you, or bankrupt you. Do not believe their hard luck stories.

Morality

Each one of us can and must have a part in raising the standard of morality before it is too late and many more lives are destroyed. Morality in this materialistic age has dropped so low throughout the world that people are losing peace of mind and well-being, and trust and hope, through utter selfishness and the 'I want, I get' attitude.

The standard of morality, and in consequence the standard of life, must be raised, so that the many individuals who recognise morality will uphold it.

Our own personal morals are extremely important. Each one of us can help to lift the standard of life.

Young people often lack morality because they are against 'normal society', they are determined to be 'different' from their families and surroundings, they wish to shock. Many of these young people 'sow their wild oats' for a few years and then become normal members of society.

Others, however, go too far and destroy their lives with riotous living, alcoholism and/or drugs. They realise almost too late the effect on their lives. Some do not realise until it is too late to turn back and severe physical and mental changes have occurred.

These are the tragic cases. However, with the right help, even these cases *can* be 'turned back', and live happy, useful lives.

Moral values are certainly something we can all put on our personal agenda today.

The breakdown of marriages plays a significant part in moral behaviour.

It seems appalling that in this present century, especially in the western world, there are so many 'gym-slip' pregnancies. Moral standards should begin to be taught at the very earliest age, in the home and in the school, for boys and girls. It always seems to be the girls who take the blame and responsibility. This should not be so. The blame should be equally distributed between the sexes. The boy is just as responsible as the girl.

It would be much better to have specially trained counsellors to visit schools to give sex and moral lessons, than for people who have little knowledge to try to teach this vitally important subject to future generations.

Many young people are rebels. They always have been, but more so today, with their new-found 'freedom'.

They usually think they are clever in rejecting conventionality, in order to shock their elders.

Many of these young people become fine citizens as they mature and realise the folly of their ways.

What about the ones who remain rebellious? Nothing very much will change them. Some land in prison, or just drift through life, believing in nothing and acting as if they don't care for anyone or anything.

Only they themselves can decide to reform them. Some will, some won't.

Self Discipline

People today, the world over, seem to lack self-discipline. It seems to have gone almost completely out of fashion.

Without self-discipline the whole structure of life for individuals, families and the world, will fall apart – as it seems to be doing.

Children in schools should be taught self-discipline as a subject. It should be practised from cradle to grave. The home is where it should also be taught, from a very early age.

Happiness is never 'bought' by other people's unhappiness. It never was and never will be.

Today it seems to be 'I want', 'I have', or 'I get'. Never mind how or who is involved.

Each individual makes a difference to the world. People never realise this. Good behaviour and thought breeds more good behaviour and thought.

Selfishness seems to be rampant. Like a forest fire – destroying so much as it 'burns on', individuals, families and countries.

Manners seem to have become almost completely unfashionable. The strange thing about manners is that so many people respond very favourably when someone shows manners.

For example, if one pulls up one's car to let another pass, that the person in the other car lifts up their hand in a 'thank you' gesture, it gives one a pleasant feeling that the small gesture on both sides was worthwhile.

When someone holds a door open, rather than letting it go into someone else's body or face, a 'thank you' is usually well received. Small gestures but they begin to add up.

If only married people and families would be polite

and have good manners within the home, it would be a refreshing breeze blowing through the home. Children would soon pick them up and manners would be a part of their lives.

Pendulums swing – but when they swing away from 'devastation' a new beginning comes again, and there is every indication that it will in the not far distant future; we must be fully aware and not respond in ways that have taken place in the past.

Everything should be used and enjoyed in moderation. When the Puritan or Prohibition periods took place, so much went under cover. This caused dishonesty, cheating, deception etc. None of these extremes is good for anyone, or countries. No persons nor governments should impose stupid restrictions. These breed unhappiness and deceit.

Forgiving

Why is it that some people seem unable to forgive? What is it in their characters, make-up or past childhood which gives them this awful 'chip on their shoulder', why are they unable to forgive? They make other people's lives a misery by their unforgiving attitude, by dragging up the 'cause' time and time again, often throughout their lives. They usually destroy what could have been happiness; happy relationships are destroyed. The person who needed to be forgiven has no doubt felt remorse for their 'sins', whatever they may have been. It is not only the one who 'sinned' who suffers indefinitely from this unforgiving attitude; others – innocent victims, have to take the backlash from the unforgiving person and the continued remorse from the unforgiven person. This can cause a devastatingly unhappy and quite unnecessary life-long 'penury'. It can cause countless unhappy situations in all sorts of domestic and even business relationships, which have nothing to do with the real situation at all. It is like a snowball, gathering pebbles and stones on its relentless journey forward.

Mental and physical 'illnesses' are often caused through this sort of situation. One usually does not realise this and would not dream that it was the cause, even of deep illness such as stomach ulcers, rheumatic types of illness, heart conditions, skin rashes and complaints, which can all be caused by these unhappy conditions.

It is very difficult to get emotionally close to anyone who has hatred and unforgiveness in their hearts. It is like a poison eating into them, usually it shows in their features and their whole attitude to life and others. They wonder why they are not liked, perhaps not given invitations when others receive them, ignored by people they would like to be friendly with.

These are the more severe cases of the hatred and unforgiving nature.

For heaven's sake, learn to forgive! Everyone will benefit, yourself, and the one you have forgiven – that must be the end of the whole unhappy episode.

Happiness

Happiness is very elusive.

Happiness is what everyone seeks but so few seem to find. When it is found, it seems in many cases to be very fleeting.

Happy is what we are all supposed and wish to be.

Happiness is of course interpreted in many ways. What makes some people happy does not necessarily make others so.

To some, money brings happiness. To others, it certainly does not.

We say: if only this, that or the other happened, I should be happy. If this were so, we would often go ahead and go after the particular changes that we thought would make us happy. However, it often happens that when we have found what we thought was going to make us happy, it may for a time, but then evaporates again, and once more we find ourselves trying to find the elusive 'something' which we hope will make us happy.

We very rarely find our happiness through possessions and often not through other human beings.

We are all too individual. Happiness can never be found through other people's unhappiness.

One can never buy happiness. If you give happiness to others, you are more likely to be able to find happiness yourself.

If you truly love someone and the love is returned, this can bring great happiness – no matter what position in life one has.

A baby or a child's smile can warm the heart and bring happiness.

The feeling that someone cares can make even an invalid happy. A word of encouragement to someone, struggling with a difficult problem, can make the difference between unhappiness and happiness.

Happiness means different things to different people. Some people find it in small things in life. The song of a bird, a baby's laughter. Loving thoughts from people can cause great happiness.

Others, however, especially people who have had difficulties in life, who have been hurt as children or adults and perhaps feel rejected and unloved – these people find it very difficult to be happy, or to feel any happiness within themselves. Often they have to have happiness 'thrown at them' before they can be touched by kindness or love of any sort. These people can also find it extremely difficult to give happiness to others.

Once these people's 'inner sanctuary' can be reached and touched, they can begin to respond to normal happiness. It is well worth the trouble, however many setbacks one might meet, to be able to replace apathy, hopelessness etc. with even a smattering of happiness. It is more than well worthwhile.

> *How beautiful upon the mountains are the feet of him that bringeth good tidings.*
> *(Isaiah 52:7)*

No one can do more good than one who brings 'good tidings' and happiness to individuals or the world, to known or unknown people. It is a commodity that needs to be enlarged to a tremendous degree, to encompass all peoples of the world.

Is happiness ever bought with other people's unhappiness? No, this is not possible. It may seem so, for a while, but gradually there creeps into one's consciousness doubt and fear. Never try to 'buy' your happiness with others' unhappiness – it never works and may react very badly on the one trying to do this to others.

What everyone needs is a 'purpose in life'. To feel needed, wanted, useful. There are tremendous opportunities in life now, to do interesting and productive things.

To sit in front of the television for hour after hour is soul destroying. It can become an obsession and cut one off from normal existence. It may take a big effort, but do this before it is too late. Others may need your help in this direction.

Get them interested in other things.

Real happiness is found within oneself.

However, the task of the individuals is to use their talents to help those nearest at hand – their family, friends and acquaintances.

If one is a shop assistant – serving someone – what a difference a nice smile makes. It lights up the face of the one smiling, and passes on a feeling of well being to the recipient. To do one's job with a feeling of pleasure, however humble it may be, to smile and be pleasant, can make a world of difference to all concerned.

Diamonds

Human beings are like diamonds. When light shines on a diamond, it has innumerable coloured facets. Human character can be likened to diamonds.

Some diamonds have more and better facets than others. It is the same with human character.

Characters, like diamonds, can be polished and their better facets brought out.

Cleaning out old character traits can be a big step forward. After the cleaning comes the polishing. Each facet can be individually polished.

Many people find it difficult to express themselves. This can happen because of their childhood. If children are not talked to as babies, they can find it almost impossible to respond normally as they grow up.

A baby should be picked up and cuddled and talked to from the earliest possible time. Certainly before they are old enough to respond – a few days or weeks old is ideal. Smiles and laughter are great healers for babies.

For any age, a spontaneous 'snatched kiss' can work wonders for morale. Often people, husband or wife, feel rejected – probably without reason – but a snatched kiss, even at the kitchen sink, can make them come alive and realise that they are not being rejected at all.

People need and want to be loved. Sometimes it may be extremely difficult to love some characters. However, if you can manage to, there is usually a great change in the 'old character'. Even their appearance seems to change.

It is never too late for renewal – to start again on a right footing.

Caring

Caring is the best way to give happiness to all ages. The mere fact that a person can feel that someone cares for or about them, gives a feeling of being wanted, needed, and this itself brings happiness.

When asked what makes one happy, there are many different answers, like the facets of a diamond. Some say 'life in general'. I think that these people must be the luckier ones in life, who have not had too many setbacks and changes in their lives. I wouldn't say that they belong to the majority.

People shouldn't think that it is only children who need a feeling of being cared for.

All people need a feeling of being cared for.

People behave in strange ways and because of this, sometimes give the impression of not caring for someone – perhaps someone who they loved previously. This change of attitude makes the person feel rejected and this has quite a devastating emotional effect on the person, and also on the one who has changed.

If one can get through to the person who has caused the offence, great changes can take place and happiness return. However, this is not always possible, as the one who has changed objects to interference. Quite often they place the blame for their odd behaviour on the one they have changed towards – making the innocent one feel guilty.

If it is impossible to get through to the one who has changed, which often is the case, one must compromise and lead one's own life to the very best of one's ability. Otherwise they will be dragged into the mire with the one who has changed. Quite a lot of strength and faith is needed to resist being dragged down. One has to cling to faith and interests.

Get new interests if possible, but don't be dragged down. Unhappiness, ill health and eventually an untimely death may take place.

It is not 'kindness' to allow anyone to drag one down, and one certainly wouldn't be thanked for it.

If only humanity, people, *ourselves,* would live to care about others, how wonderful it would be.

The cab driver, the baker, the business executive, the home-maker, the teacher, the salesperson, the secretary, the farmer, everyone, has a unique opportunity to use individual skills and talents for the benefit of humanity. This would do more good in the world than one could imagine.

A world in need, people in need, respond as burdens are lifted. Hearts let go of their hardness, hope is created. The world of the individual suddenly looks brighter.

The world begins to exude comfort, peace, joy and vitality.

There is no need to agonise over all the good that needs to be done, to despair because there is so much wrong. Such attitudes would be self-defeating and would hold back our own contribution.

Our own contribution, however small, can start to snowball.

There is only one way – that is, *Do It*.

Never make invalids or elderly people feel a burden to you. If they actually are, get help. If you have no family able or willing to help, get it from outside the family. Contact the authorities. Go to the nearest Citizens Advice Bureau and they will put you in touch with people able to help. Never despair. It reacts very badly on people who cannot help themselves.

Envy

There should be no envy and no rivalry. Everyone has his or her own niche in the spiritual universe. Each one's identity is distinct and completely his or her own. We are all individuals.

Everyone is essential to the wholeness of God's universe.

This is certainly a very difficult concept for us to understand and accept, with all the difficulties of this world.

To realise how much one has, especially in the Western world, can help to eliminate envy of others' possessions.

Most people go through mild forms of envy occasionally in their lives. This can be easy to deal with and is not in the same class as jealousy. It must still not be allowed to develop but must be quickly eliminated.

Jealousy

Jealousy is like a festering sore. It eats into people's characters. It causes untold agonies of unhappiness, not only in the one who is jealous or the one they are jealous of, but in the many surrounding victims – people whose lives are touched and even ruined by this vice.

It can attack people like a snake in the grass, rearing its ugly head when least expected.

Unkind words can cut very deeply into people, especially sensitive people. Jealousy can make grave scars where there should be no scars. It can also cause trouble between quite innocent people. Misunderstandings are rife where jealousy is concerned.

More often than not, jealousy can be caused by a feeling of insecurity in the jealous person who needs help and understanding. Not always a very easy task for the ones willing to help.

Jealousy is like a disease, it will develop into chronic phases and cause chronic unhappiness for the jealous person and others who are the recipients of the jealousy, and also others who may come into contact with either side. It is something which seems to have tentacles like an octopus (apologies to the octopus!) and will spread if not checked.

The jealous people may not be aware that their feelings are of jealousy, and the recipients may also be unaware that the strange behaviour is because of jealousy. It causes tremendous unhappiness – and illness, if not checked.

People who are not directly connected with either party – sometimes children, can pick up the unhappy threads of what is going on around them. In the home, office, anywhere, people's lives are not only made miserable but can be completely destroyed by their own or others' jealousy.

Jealousy is an evil which eats into people, depriving them often of all decency, altering their characters, often their features. They take on an almost sour look.

Jealousy can cause crimes of many sorts and destroys human lives.

How does one overcome jealousy?

Firstly the jealous one has to realise and accept the fact that they are jealous. Some will not face this and put all the blame on others. They consider they are perfect and everyone else is to blame. These people are probably best left to their own devices because one usually just wastes one's breath trying to convince them.

The ones who can be helped, who respond to others, are the ones well worth helping. It is usually extremely difficult for them to face the problem. It can be almost a defect in their characters. They can be helped to become altered characters.

If they will accept that they are jealous, get them to write a list of all the 'plus' things they have in their own lives. Help them to do this.

If friends or family cannot help, they may need counselling from special organisations.

The Greener Grass

One always thinks that the grass is greener on the other side of the fence. This is usually a myth. One never seems to take into account other people's setbacks and struggles. Although many seem to put a very good face on everything it might be that their lives are not so good at all.

It is quite amazing the length people will often go to, to put a good face on things. To hide the facts from the outside world. This often takes a great deal of courage, but is often well worth the struggle.

Do not always long to be on the other side of the fence; be grateful for what you have.

Relationships

The warmth and security of a happy relationship surpasses all trials and tribulations.

A happy relationship is built up of mutual trust. Forgiveness for misdemeanours is absolutely necessary for forming a good relationship. No one is perfect and one should realise and accept this fact. When one has forgiven, whatever it may have been, great or small, it may never be forgotten, but it must never, ever, be thrown up, or even brought up in anger or conversation. Once it has been forgiven, it must be 'put away' for ever.

Many relationships are wrecked because of the continual reminder of 'what you did', or said etc.

The putting away for ever is an absolute must – if you cannot do this – then end the relationship or marriage. Don't drag on. It will end eventually under these circumstances, and cause endless unhappiness in the meantime.

Do not compare yourself with anyone else. You are completely individual, 'you are you', and no one else. Follow the best in others, if you feel uncertain – but no comparisons.

Forcing Personality On Another

Some people impose themselves and their personality on others.
Many people want others, especially partners, to be as they want them to be and not as they are.
It is often very difficult for the person being imposed upon to overcome this. If this happens to you, make this other person realise that you are a person in your own right, that you have your own personality that objects to being forced to be someone alien. It is not easy. Many people put up with someone overbearing because they want to avoid confrontation. The longer it goes on, the more difficult it becomes to overcome it. But this must be done, in the nicest possible way. If they will not respond to this confrontation, then a firmer way must be found, even asking someone else to help, preferably someone who knows both of you.

Assurance

The word 'assurance' is a gentle word. A word of hope, of something being sure. No doubts can creep in, no fears, a feeling of trust, leading to well being.

Many people, in many walks of life, have the opportunity to be able to give 'assurance'. It can be tremendously helpful. It is a word which so many people world-wide need, from governments to individual people of all ages.

The power of suggestion is very powerful in the human mind. Wonderful and powerful forces can be put into operation.

Physical health and spiritual health go hand in hand.

Health

There are many different ways of healing.

One can always find one which relates best to an individual.

Orthodox medicine, non-medicinal, herbal, acupuncture, Christian Science, spiritual healing and many others can help.

Find the one which you feel best with and give it a very good chance of healing you. You can change your mind, several times if you wish, but not before giving a very good chance to the method you choose.

I don't think that anyone should be made to feel guilty – whatever their belief – about the choice they make. One must never be made to feel guilty about the treatment they choose. Patients, helpers etc. can be caused great distress which is most detrimental to everything and everyone concerned. No one should try to put any pressure on anyone, despite their own beliefs. We are all complete individuals and no one else, except God, knows our 'inner selves'.

There are many types of healing and each individual must find the one most suitable to his or her needs. Change several times if necessary. If you find one that is suitable to you and relatives or friends try to dissuade you – don't be dissuaded, stay with the one you consider most helpful. There are so many different ways of having help.

Never accept what seems to be a hopeless diagnosis as final. Hold on to hope and follow where it leads you, willing and praying to be well.

There is a 'doctor' within you. It is the healing power of nature within you. Never give up hope, always look forward and 'know' that you will be well and full of life again.

Never be fanatical, be flexible in all things.

Feeling 'Down'

When you are feeling 'down' or depressed, what is the best thing to do about it? The best thing to do is to get a piece of paper and write down all the good and positive things that you have, and that have happened to you in life. The negative things will then almost certainly be wiped out. You will realise that life is pretty good after all! Persist in keeping good things in the forefront of your mind, however much the bad things try to push them aside – do not let them! Tell Satan, 'Get thee behind me!' Keep smiling. It is amazing how a smile helps everyone, especially yourself. The creases in your face go into the right places!

However, if a deep depression persists, see someone about it, medical etc. If anyone is in this state, it is dangerous to tell them to 'pull themselves together', because without appropriate help they cannot do so. The depression has become an illness which needs to be treated professionally. Nothing can be worse for these sufferers than to be told to 'snap out of it', it only makes the condition worse. Get the right help, as soon as possible.

Dishonesty

Dishonesty starts usually in small beginnings.
Stealing a small article in a shop or superstore and having 'got away with it' makes one 'braver' for the next thing to steal.
Some people continue, until it becomes an obsession.
There are many reasons why people succumb to this. It can be through lack of love, depression or mental breakdown.
However, this is not usually the case. Greed, money for drugs etc are very prevalent today.
Children must be stopped and punished for stealing at the earliest opportunity, before it gets a hold on them. They know full well what they are doing is wrong.
In some cases medical counselling or psychiatric help is needed, instead of fines or prison.

Despair

I wonder how many people have reached the rock bottom of despair. Many may feel they have, but the real, deep, hopeless despair is when there is no way – or seems no way – out of the dilemma.

The utter basic hopelessness is soul destroying, one feeling this way can see no hope whatsoever. These are the ones who decide to take an overdose, or other means, as a way out. The only hope for these people is *if* there is someone who reaches them in time. Even strangers can save their lives. The Samaritans are a life line.

There are various reasons for people reaching this terrible bottomless pit of hopeless despair. It can be caused by a depressive illness which needs definite medical, or similar, help.

Despair can be caused, and often is, by other people's lack of understanding, and not caring what they do to others.

The ones at the receiving end of these peoples' actions need help and understanding. Where do they get this? There are not many people who can be trusted with one's inner feelings. Never tell people your troubles unless you are completely convinced that they can be trusted not to 'tell anyone else in confidence'. This second person would be likely to go around telling others what they know of so-and-so.

Do be absolutely certain of the person you tell your troubles to, otherwise contact the Samaritans, or some other professional person. You can speak to them in complete confidence and they will give you advice, or put you in contact with the people who will be able to help you. This advice is for all levels of despair.

Suicide

People who get to the state of despair and commit suicide are the ones who don't care what happens to themselves afterwards. If they knew that they had to work out their problems on the other side, they would probably still end it all on this planet. They get in such deep despair, that all they can think about is ending it all.

Some may not 'end it all', only do severe damage to themselves which they may have to live with for the rest of their lives, for example brain damage from overdoses, or physical damage caused by throwing themselves from heights or under traffic.

I hope that no one reading this will ever resort to any of these 'ending all' devices. Please, please think again. You can always get help – whatever mess you are in.

There is a Higher Power who will respond to your prayers for help. Many people who have reached the depths of despair, some many times, have come out of their despair and have been led back into very happy and productive lives.

Do please be one of these people. We need people who know what despair is like. It is much more character building than forever living in 'Disneyland'. People who have suffered become more understanding, tolerant and helpful to others who need this help.

One need not have the experience of very deep despair to become a much more tolerant and understanding person.

Many people take an overdose as a cry for help. Please, please cry for help before the overdose. Call the Samaritans, doctor, relatives or friends. You can always get help.

Never doubt this.

Apathy

Apathy can be soul destroying. Many things can bring it on, circumstances, people, depression etc. The main thing is to recognise it, then it can be quite easily eliminated.

The main answer to apathy is 'Do something.'

Sometimes it would seem we have to run into a brick wall before we awake from our apathy and realise that nothing is being done. One is at a standstill or going backwards.

Do things, you never know what you can do until you try.

There is a tremendous need in this world for people to do things no one need be apathetic and feel useless.

Make sure that the apathy is not caused by some illness.

Avoid a 'can't be bothered' attitude in life. This causes negative reactions, which are to be avoided for a healthy, happy life.

The time spent doing what you felt you couldn't be bothered to do will be well spent, and you will have a feeling of achievement and freedom.

You don't know what you can do until you try.

Take trouble, don't always try to take the 'easy way out'. Taking trouble usually pays dividends. This applies to all things in life, business, personal hygiene, dress and help for others.

You will find that the more you do, the more you can do.

If you feel 'you haven't go the time', do something. It is surprising how much time you have when you have done something!

Killing – Murder – Wars

People do not kill each other – how can they kill something that is eternal? They just kill the body and cause the real spiritual being to pass over to the next sphere – before they are ready to go. This causes great distress to the loved ones left behind – who also do not understand that there is no death, only a 'passing on'.

If people understood this, there would be no killing as such. The fact that the people who do the killing have to face the reality of their terrible deeds here or hereafter, is not understood by the majority of people.

Tragedy

How does one face tragedy, like the death of a loved one, perhaps a child, or a very close relative, and keep a feeling that there is a life ahead?
Each case is a completely different one – no two people are alike in their reactions.
The death of a young husband or wife leaves the other behind, probably with a young family and the prospects of a lonely life.
Friendship at this time is a wonderful help.
Prayer can help to heal the grief, to know that although our loved ones are not with us, they are not very far away. They have 'passed on', Not died, and we will meet again.
Our loved ones would wish us to continue our own lives as normally as possible. Realise this and go forward step by step.
There are many groups who are trained in counselling for bereavement.

Being Impulsive

By being impulsive you can make terrible mistakes. Don't be afraid to accept the fact that you may be behaving impulsively.

Stay back and look the problem squarely in the face. Admit that you could be impulsive, and that it would be better to halt a while and think again, when the heat of the battle has cooled off. This gives you a chance to weigh things up and see everything in a better, more constructive way.

Don't be afraid to do this. It is being sensible and adult, and will save you perhaps years of regret and unhappiness.

Boredom

Boredom is soul destroying. It is in fact a state of mind. It must be because when one realises that the world is absolutely full of things to occupy one, how can one be bored, unless it is a state of mind.

When you read about the people who have terrible deformities, blindness, paralysis etc. who are achieving wonderful things despite their handicaps, it must make one feel ashamed to be bored in this wonderful world. There are so many things one can and should do to make one's life worthwhile, as well as helping others. Do make up your mind to snap out of the boredom and become productive in some way.

Boredom can cause conflicts, hopelessness, deceitfulness, in fact it can completely destroy what could be a useful, loving and beautiful character. It can cause depression, hopelessness and defeatism, and push people on to alcohol or drugs.

There are people who do not want help, whatever realities are put before them, they reject everything as if you are quite mental to believe in anything at all.

Why are these people so egotistical, so full of their own importance, so unbelieving? We shall never really know. What goes on in their minds is a mystery. It is quite impossible to get through to them. It is almost a waste of time even trying.

There are the genuinely mentally ill, psychopaths, schizophrenics, manic depressives and others, mostly curable, illnesses. These people all need help.

It does not really matter what happens in life, if there isn't anything – no God nor eternity. But it does matter if there is, *and there is.*

The real spiritual characters of people are unchanged forever in their individuality, though they are governed by one Principle.

However, like diamonds, they can be polished and go through stages of learning, to become eventually perfect.

The trouble is in many cases that people of different religions and denominations and sects, seem to believe that only their way of thinking and believing is right, and that everyone else is wrong. It is their dogmatic approach that is wrong – everyone is right when they follow the belief in Deity or God.

Religious wars would cease, and would never have been, if only people throughout the world would believe and follow this.

The sun shines on the just and unjust without discrimination, no one is excluded from its warmth and light.

Deity or God pours out love for all.

Divine Intelligence does not include much or little, more or less, according to human standards. It is immeasurable, inexhaustible. God's loving kindness goes beyond any measurement, it is infinite, has no end. It never ceases under any circumstances.

To be conscious of His love, we need to reject whatever would tempt us to disbelieve in God, and then go forward to live in obedience to Divine Law.

There is a right and wrong way of doing everything – why not find the right way?

There is an answer to everything – let us find the right answer and act upon it.

Lies can never be right – let us face up to the truth. Lies breed more lies.

Fanaticism

Do not be a fanatic about anything. Fanaticism can ruin your life and that of others. Be reasonable, more elastic, able to see others' points of view, accepting others' points of view.

Fanaticism can destroy normal relationships and life. If you feel fanatical, conquer it. If you need help to do this, seek it in the right direction, but do conquer it before it gets a hold.

Be flexible not fanatical.

Rejection

Rejection in any form, even in thoughts, can be devastating to the one rejected. Whatever age one may be, the impact can be disastrous.

Tiny babies, only days old, can sense rejection and react to it, even refusing food.

A look of rejection can be spotted by the recipient. If you have to reject someone, or something, do it in the kindest possible way.

Pity

Pity is one of the most unfortunate words in the disctionary. No one, just no one, likes being pitied. It makes one feel small, insignificant, and sometimes very aggressive – even trapped. One longs to throw off the 'offending garment' of whatever the trouble or illness is.
Please, please, never pity anyone. It can cause a self-destructive tendency.
It is a completely negative word. No one needs or wants this.

Be Constructive

One can feel sorry for people, but do so in a constructive way. Never look down on another person, whether they are suffering through illness, tragedy, business failure or some other reason. You can let them know how sorry you are – but never pity them.

Existence

Why are some people given enormous wealth, high positions, good health, good fortune? We do not know the answers in this present existence.

However, there must certainly be an answer and a reason.

We have to work out our own lives to the best of our ability, within the position we are given, in this present existence. I am certain that what we do with our present 'lives' is consistent with what happens to us in our next and future existences.

The answer comes that we are working through our destiny, as we have in previous lives, which no doubt predestines the existence we are now in on this materialistic planet.

God has given us free will. We use it as we will.

If we knew about our previous existences and the fact that we continue on eternally, it would perhaps not let our true personalities have full scope, we should probably spend our lives pretending to be what we are not. As it is, we are showing our true selves, not always to our advantage! However, we are working through our best and worst selves, for better or worse in our next existence.

People say, why should we think that there is another existence after this one? No one has ever come back to tell us.

This is not true at all. As I have mentioned previously thousands upon thousands of people have had all sorts of experiences of past relatives and friends returning with messages in some way. Many of these people are afraid to tell of these experiences because the people who have not had such experiences themselves ridicule them and consider them to be peculiar. This is a great pity because a lot of good could come out of these experiences and great progress could be made. People would be less afraid of dying, would be free to go forward, looking ahead, knowing that life is eternal, instead of the terrible uncertainty which the majority of people suffer in this world.

If human beings are not able to give adequate answers to these problems, why don't we listen to Deity? You may say, how do we know that there is a God? Well, why not let us give Him a chance? For decades many people in the world have been trying to live without God, and just look what a mess we have got ourselves, and the world, into.

So why not let us try another way? Why not let us turn over a new leaf, and give God a chance? This is what He is asking us to do, so let us do it, before it is too late and we have destroyed ourselves and what could be a wonderful world. You may say, how do we begin?

First of all, let's try to have some faith – even as a 'mustard seed'. I read this somewhere and copied it into my diary.

> *Give me, O Lord, a grain*
> *of faith,*
> *that it may grow, like*
> *the mustard seed*
> *to a sturdy plant of*
> *Christ-like trust and*
> *understanding.*
> *Where healing truths*
> *may come to lodge*
> *within its branches.*

In his book *In Tune With The Infinite*, Ralph Waldo Trine states –

*When we open ourselves to the highest inspirations,
they never fail us.*

LOVE

We have been given the ability to love, also to hate. Hate causes destruction, envy and all the negative thoughts, feelings and actions in the world – all the destructive forces.

Love counteracts evil and destruction. One may say, I just find it too difficult to love so-and-so.

If one sits down and really thinks about the person one hates and starts to think of some good things about them, which must be in this person, it is surprising how one's feelings can gradually change. Forces in the world are not static – they travel the globe. If one can have a change of attitude to the person one hates, it is quite astounding how the other person can change. Many situations have completely changed when one kind word has been spoken, even after many years of animosity, whole relationships have been altered for the better.

Love and Forgiving

Love is connected with forgiving. No one can lead a happy life if they cannot forgive. It is absolutely essential to one's well being. It may be very difficult indeed, particularly if one has been badly treated. One may never see the person to be forgiven, they may even have 'passed on', but the fact of forgiving makes a tremendous difference to the one who has forgiven. Try it and see! It also makes a tremendous difference to the one forgiven, if they are still with us, it can change their lives for the better. It can change their personalities.

The forgiving person looks and feels a free person. It releases the best in our characters.

I am sure that if one forgives a person who has passed on (died), this forgiveness can be transmitted to the person 'beyond the grave', to the next dimension of existence. I believe that this can be known, and the person on the 'other side' will be greatly helped.

Children are not born with hate, they are born with love.

Hate can soon be passed on to children, although it is not their own characteristic. For example, the children in Northern Ireland and some countries in the Middle East are often brought up to hate, but when they are allowed to meet or go to school with a different religious denomination, they find they like each other! What dreadful things human beings are, inflicting our prejudices upon other human beings, without giving them a chance to even know the people they hate and fear. So much destruction is caused by people who want power, at any cost – except to themselves.

Love, Peace, Happiness

The one thing that could heal the world is *Love*.

If only people would change their attitudes and love instead of hate or showing indifference, the world would become an entirely different place. Families would become united. Peoples of the world would become happy and thoughtful and loving too.

The words in the Bible which David spoke, *Be still and know that I am God*, have a wonderful healing effect on one's mind and body. It takes hate away, and in its place is a feeling of peace and harmony – on the way to loving.

Peace and happiness are what we *all* long for, people of every nation, every religion, every individual. How can one find peace if there is animosity in the hearts of men and women and nations? No peace can be found in this way, nor happiness.

The Apostle Paul's advice:

> *Finally, brethren, whatsoever things are true, whatsoever things are honest, whatsoever things are just, whatsoever things are pure, whatsoever things are lovely, whatsoever things are of good report; if there be any virtue, and if there be any praise, think on these things.*
>
> *(Philippians 4:8)*

Paul is giving good advice here. If we follow his recommendations faithfully, there ceases to be even an opportunity for a bad mood. How simple this advice – and yet how difficult!

It is the Power of God that offers us peace, as nothing else can.

Paul's Message to the Corinthians (1 Cor 13)

> *Though I speak with the tongues of men and of angels, and have not love, I am become as sounding brass, or a tinkling cymbal. And though I have the gift of prophecy, and understand all mysteries, and all knowledge; and though I have all faith, so that I could remove*

mountains, and have not love, I am nothing. And though I bestow all my goods to feed the poor, and though I give my body to be burned, and have not love, it profiteth me nothing.

*Love suffereth long, and is kind;
Love envieth not;
Love vaunteth not itself, is not puffed up,
Doth not behave itself unseemly,
Seeketh not her own,
Is not easily provoked,
Thinketh no evil;*

Rejoiceth not in iniquity, but rejoiceth in the truth; Beareth all things, believeth all things, hopeth all things, endureth all things.

Love never faileth; but whether there be prophecies, they shall fail; whether there be tongues, they shall cease; whether there be knowledge, it shall vanish away. For we know in part, and we prophesy in part. But when that which is perfect is come, then that which is in part shall be done away.

When I was a child, I spake as a child, I understood as a child, I thought as a child: but when I became a man, I put away childish things. For now we see through a glass, darkly; but then face to face: now I know in part; but then shall I know even as also I am known. And now abideth faith, hope, love, these three; but the greatest of them is love.

'Where love is,' said Tolstoy, 'God is,' and we might add, where God and love are, there is happiness. So a practical principle in creating happiness is to practise love.

ON AFFAIRS OF MANKIND

Actions and Influences of Thought

Humanity is at present living in an existence, or plane, of law and control, where malice, hate and envy are as antagonistic to the physical and mental well being as poison would be.

If you want to save yourself, your life, from unhappiness, sorrow and pain, do all you can to stop hating, having resentment and bitterness. Learn to forgive, to love, to be kind and show mercy to other individuals.

Love and kindness will transform you and your character. It will alter your whole personality and even the way you look, both men and women.

Why have we put hatred in the place of love and believed illogical untruths about existence?

The misery, unhappiness and poverty which people suffer are completely unnecessary. God's universe is unlimited in every way. There are no limits to anything. It is only what people have done to each other, and the world, which causes limitations.

God gave us unlimited life, goodness and love. Why has the world not accepted this, but abandoned it for hopelessness, sickness and greed?

Do let us think deeply on these things so that we can

transform our lives and those of others, and eventually the world.

There is too much negative thinking about life. Consciously or unconsciously, the people in the world today base their thinking on limitation. Limited income, limited opportunity, limited health, limited time etc.

Negative thinking can be turned around into brighter, happier, more expansive and constructive thoughts. This would bring a correction in our way of thinking and can turn life around.

I'll do it 'My Way'

This is the only way to be true to yourself, if it is the correct way and does not hurt anyone. It is no use trying to follow other people's ways, unless they really suit you. Do it your own way, find out about things and follow what inspires you.

If you cannot find your own way, pray to God about it and follow His guidance. This is possible when you are genuine and not half-hearted and believe that this can happen. Determine to go forward, and don't discuss it with unbelievers.

This can relate to almost any project in life. You must know within yourself that the way you want to go is the right way for you, and will not hurt anyone else.

Be positive, realise the marvellous things we should be grateful for in this present century. The aeroplane, which can take us to the remotest parts of the globe, was unthought of a century ago. Many, many other blessings, communication by telephone which, apart from easier business, enables us to feel closer to loved ones who may be many thousands of miles away. Counting your blessings is a wonderful healing process.

Fears

One of the greatest scourges of mankind today, and probably always has been, is fear.

Fear itself often causes worse happenings. One can become over protective to oneself and others and one's children.

Fear causes devastation in countries, as well as in people's individual lives.

Fears are so numerous, it would be impossible to list them all. From fear of the dark as children, into fear of war as adults, of murder, rape, losing possessions, or even partners.

The way to eliminate fear is to trust God. To have faith and to pray. It is remarkable how the power of prayer can eliminate fear.

If one fears, for no specific reason, it may be that some fear from the past, one's childhood, has become deeply rooted in the mind, even though the cause may have been forgotten. A child can become so terrified of some happening that it gets buried in the subconscious. A happening in later life may bring it to the surface. If it is not possible to deal oneself with the consequences of this, outside help may be required. If this is so, do not hesitate to seek professional help, so that you can be 'free' of this and lead a free and happy life in the future.

Fear can make one ill, and can kill, through illness. Overcome fear and your body and mind will begin to respond normally.

We have been given dominion over everything that harasses us. Learn this, and it will be the end of fear, and the beginning of health and happiness.

Confidence

Almost everyone lacks confidence in some form or another at some time during their lives.

Often lack of confidence is formed in childhood, for various reasons, and unfortunately continues during one's lifetime, for many gathering momentum as the years progress.

It is good to know that one need not be burdened by this malady, but that there are many and various ways of obtaining help.

There are many people who are professionally trained to help – medical and non-medical. There are many books on the subject which can be a tremendous help. One must study these and not just read them.

Six books which can be tremendously helpful if studied are books which have helped innumerable people throughout the world. They are:

First and foremost the Bible.

Science and Health with Key to the Scriptures by Mary Baker Eddy.

In Tune with the Infinite by Ralph Waldo Trine.

The Power of Positive Thinking by Norman Vincent Peale. He has written many books.

Power Through Constructive Thinking by Dr Emmet Fox. He has also written many books.

Life is for Living by Patience Strong. A very easy to read quite small book.

If you go to a library or book shop and ask the assistant on books associated with confidence. I am sure the assistant will recommend many.

There are many helpful thoughts spoken and written centuries ago, that are just as true today and will be forever. The Bible tells us of man's divine heritage.

> *Behold, what manner of love the Father hath bestowed upon us, that we should be called the sons of God . . . Beloved, now are we the sons of God.*
>
> *(1 John 3:1-2)*

Think what it means to be the sons of God NOW! The Scriptures do not say that at some future time, or through some process, we shall become the sons of God, but that this is our present state of being.

To achieve the understanding of our present status as the sons of God, we must establish our authority for such a conclusion. We find this authority in many statements in the Bible. In the *Book of Genesis (1:26)* we read: *God said, Let us make man in our image, after our likeness.*

As God is Spirit, His image and likeness must be spiritual.

Paul wrote in his *Epistle to the Romans (8:16-17) The Spirit itself beareth witness with our spirit, that we are the children of God: and if children, then heirs; heirs of God, and joint-heirs with Christ.*

No greater heritage could be bestowed upon us. Does not this verify our status as the Sons of God?

If you or I, or anybody, think constantly of the forces that seem to be against us, we will build them up into a power far beyond that which is justified. They will assume a formidable strength which they do not actually possess. But if on the contrary, you mentally visualise and affirm and reaffirm your assets, and keep your thoughts on them, emphasising them to the fullest extent, you will rise out of any difficulty regardless of what it may be.

Your inner powers will reassert themselves and, with the help of God, lift you from defeat to victory.

One of the most powerful concepts, one which is a sure

cure for lack of confidence, is the thought that God is actually with you and helping you. This is one of the simplest teachings in religion.

A very important statement was made by a psychiatrist. He said: 'Attitudes are more important than facts.' It is worth repeating until its truths grip you. Any fact facing us, however difficult, even seemingly hopeless, is not so important as our attitude towards that fact. How you think about a fact may defeat you before you ever do anything about it. You may permit a fact to overwhelm you mentally before you start to deal with it actually.

On the other hand, a confident and optimistic thought pattern can modify one's reaction to the fact completely.

If you feel that you are defeated and have lost confidence in your ability to win, sit down, take a piece of paper and make a list, not of the factors that are against you, but of those that are for you.

Feelings of confidence actually induce increased strength. * Basil King once said: 'Be bold, and mighty forces will come to your aid.' Experience proves the truth of this. You will feel these mighty forces aiding you as your increasing faith reconditions your attitudes.

Emerson declared a tremendous truth, 'They conquer who believe they can,' and he added, 'do the things you fear, and the death of fear is certain.' Practise confidence and faith, and your fears and insecurities will soon have no power over you.

The secret is to fill your mind with thoughts of faith, confidence and security. This will expel all thoughts of doubt, all lack of confidence.

---

* *The Power of Positive Thinking* by Norman Vincent Peale.

Confidence and fear are almost parallel: the one works on the other.

Confidence is one of the greatest assets we humans can have. Lack of confidence causes much distress in life, work and relationships.

If certain methods are followed, most people can be helped, in many cases cured.

It is important to realise that you are dealing with the most tremendous power in the world when you pray.

If you don't believe it –

Try it!

Emerson spoke of, 'The current that knows its way,' and Shakespeare said, 'There's a divinity that shapes our ends.'

If you would be carried towards your greatest good, you must trust the stream of Providence and cease to think of yourself as a piece of driftwood bobbing about on the restless and unpredictable sea of life. Know that you are in the flow of divine blessing.

'The current that knows its way.'

Below is some advice I have taken from books, books which have helped innumerable people over very many years.

There is absolutely no doubt that 'miracles' *do happen.*

The Bible says that miracles can happen, it says many times that miracles always will happen if you believe them to be possible and are willing to recognise the power of God and to call upon it.

Remember that God is our Everlasting Father.

Prayer is the greatest power available to the individual in solving problems.

It is definitely stated and is a fact, that the Highest Power can heal a person, that there is no problem, difficulty, or defeat you cannot solve or overcome by faith and prayer to God. God will help you always.

Why not draw upon that Highest Power?

'Realisation' of God is what counts. Not just thinking or talking about Him. It is realisation, as distinct from mere theorising and fine words, which is the substance of things hoped for, the evidence of things not seen.

Meanwhile, it is as well to know that all sorts of practical difficulties can be overcome by sincere prayer, without any realisation at all.

The realisation of the presence of God is a thing that no one else can do for us. We can, and should, help one another in overcoming difficulties: 'Bear ye one another's burdens' – but the realisation (or making real) of the presence of God, the 'substance' or 'evidence' can in the nature of things be had only at first hand.

The thing that means spiritual life to you is your realisation of God, here and now.

Prayer

Prayer puts us in tune with a deep spiritual reality that harmoniously corrects human problems.
Spiritual reality is free to *all*. It satisfies us. It makes us whole. It brings us peace and new energy. It gives us a solid reason for 'being'.
Human experience is a learning and proving ground.
A college student was healed through prayer. Through prayer she was helped to establish two spiritual facts as reality in her consciousness. Good – God's love – is all powerful and present in her life. Secondly, unity with good eliminates evil.

Beauty

There is only one kind of Beauty that can transcend time and many women possess it. It is Beauty of the Spirit that lights the eyes and transforms even a plain woman into a beautiful one. Women with wit, charm and warmth, who are interested in others, forget themselves and accept each stage of life gracefully, they are the lasting beauties of this world, and the happiest.

I read this somewhere many years ago and I never forget it, it is so true.

Age

People should never be called 'old people'. Words which are much more acceptable to all are 'mature people'.

Think young and progressive. Look forward to each day and the future. Leave the past behind. Not one jot of it can be altered, happy or unhappy, it has gone. We stagnate if we live in the past. The future is before us, and if we look forward to it with happiness, we are assuring a happy future, following the 'fashion' of the time, in our own individual way.

By following 'fashion' in our own individual way, we can be elegant men and women, and possess dignity which belongs to ourselves – and which others will admire.

To keep our minds young, we have to 'think' young – but not childishly.

One should create cheerfulness in thought and expression, sociability in association and inclination.

No matter how many years may seemingly have passed over one's head, no one need retire to the chimney corner.

Years should always bring wisdom, but never decrepitude.

Many of the world's famous people have done remarkable works in their eighties and nineties. John Wesley at eighty-two years of age in the midst of his activities said, 'It is now eleven years since I have felt any such thing as weariness.'

When we fully grasp the spiritual nature of man, we will experience the freedom of unlimited being. This was the message that Jesus brought to mankind.

Let no one look forward to dull, purposeless, empty and useless years, in which he or she expects to experience loneliness, weariness and inactivity.

Never feel that you are getting too old to do this or that. Age is of no concern. Think young and you will become much younger in looks and mind.

Never feel that you will not have enough time to 'do this or that'. Remember that Christ did all His work in approximately three years!

Never say I won't do it, time is too short. Attempt all things and have a go at new things. You will be surprised how this will put new energy and life into you.

Have birthdays by all means, but don't be too anxious to tell your age to others – keep them guessing!

Grandmothers and grandfathers – whether blood relations or not can be loved dearly and find new life in helping families in many ways. Children can love and become very attached to loving, smiling elderly people. Go forward!

Alfred Lord Tennyson writes:

> *Some work of Noble Note,*
> *May yet be done –*
> *'Tis not too late to seek a Newer World.*

Keep alive, keep interested. Do things. Always do your best to be cheerful and loving. The more you do, and practise this advice, the easier everything becomes.

Age should be coupled with wisdom.

Retirement

Retirement should be a time of regeneration, new interests and a feeling of going ahead. Not one of sitting back, feeling useless and a 'has been'.

To feel useless is extremely demoralising, and this feeling must not, in any circumstances, be allowed to grow, or it will become a festering sore, for oneself and family and community. Old illnesses will begin to prevail and more sinister ones appear.

All this can be prevented. After all, how can one really feel that life is finished on retirement, when life itself is eternal? It is just another stepping stone on our way.

If people are starting life again in retirement, it may be unwise to go to live in an entirely new place, which maybe you thoroughly enjoyed for holidays etc., until you have spent some time there, to find out what it would be like to live there in the winter, as well as in the summer. Also realise that it can be lonely and quite devastating to go to a new place when you do not know anyone there. Many people have done this and have bitterly regretted it. Starting life in a new place is quite different in retirement than when one is younger. Younger people meet more people and make new friends through their jobs, and if they have children, through their association with the schools and other parents. It is completely different in retirement.

Don't be anxious to abandon your old, familiar friends and places!

As you get older, you need to change. This does not mean abandoning anything in life, but just to change. For example, a vigorous activity can be changed for an art course, or any other course which seems stimulating. It can in fact awaken dormant talents, which can prove to be lucrative as well as stimulating and interesting.

Go through the list of courses at your local college. Do not be put off by the feeling 'I couldn't do it.' You can, if you try, and the effort you put into it will be repaid a hundredfold.

There are courses for both sexes, of all ages.

Human Life

Human beings are like sculptors, moulding their clay. The 'clay' is life. Some are better at it than others – brilliant. It does not matter what state of life they are in, very wealthy, medium or poor, their talent for living, 'moulding' their lives has little to do with wealth or position. Money is of course very necessary while we are in this present existence, but money itself does not create happiness, in some cases it is the reverse, particularly if it has not been earned and given too freely at an early age. Usually in this case it is not appreciated but accepted as a 'due'. It can take away a child's ambition, and because there seems nothing to work for, may cause boredom.

Boredom, as has already been mentioned, is the curse of all ages of mankind. It is a complete destroyer of character of all ages, and television can be an 'eater-away' of one's character. Dependence on watching the 'box' is one of the main curses of this generation. It deprives families of getting together, for discussions, family evenings, even seeing friends. These things may happen, but instead of lively conversations, so many sit in front of the 'box'.

It takes away one's incentive of thinking, planning, acting, it is almost a drug in itself. Be selective in your viewing.

Putting the children in front of the television, whilst parents are otherwise occupied, is wrong in many cases.

How are we going to remedy all this, and get back to life? Life as it should be lived. A wonderful, worthwhile existence. Has the world gone too far in the wrong direction?

We cannot turn back the clock, nor should we want to, to take a new direction for our lives.

We can take on a new direction whatever age, whatever nationality.

It doesn't matter how far we have gone wrong, environment, personal or other reasons, however serious, it can be stopped, altered, forgiven, if appealed to in the right way. One must be completely honest and straightforward.

People who read and study the Bible find in its inspired word a sufficient guide to eternal life.

When one gets a fair understanding of the Bible one should cease to want to fight anyone.

A Book for everyday people, in an Everyday World, who want to know Why?

Deity or God is for all people, all nationalities, not just for this or that religion, also for people who have no religion or who are uncertain about religion.

CONCLUSIONS

Sermon on the Mount (Matt 5:2-12)

And he opened his mouth, and taught them, saying,
Blessed are the poor in spirit: for theirs is the kingdom of heaven.
Blessed are they that mourn: for they shall be comforted.
Blessed are the meek: for they shall inherit the earth.
Blessed are they which do hunger and thirst after righteousness: for they shall be filled.
Blessed are the merciful: for they shall obtain mercy.
Blessed are the pure in heart: for they shall see God.
Blessed are the peacemakers: for they shall be called the children of God.
Blessed are they which are persecuted for righteousness' sake: for theirs is the kingdom of heaven.
Blessed are ye, when men shall revile you, and persecute you, and shall say all manner of evil against you falsely, for my sake.
Rejoice, and be exceeding glad: for great is your reward in heaven: for so persecuted they the prophets which were before you.

When one prays, anywhere, anytime, one must pray spiritually, not materially. How? Realise that you are basically spiritual, that this is the Real You, and that your life is eternal. However simple it may be, pray to God as your spiritual Father-Mother. It does not necessarily have to be in church, or any special place, God is in constant contact with all His people.

Why Now?

Because *this* generation, with all the marvellous things which have been given us, is getting itself, individually and collectively, and the world, into an awful mess, and it doesn't seem able to find its way out. Mainly because it is trying *without* God.

REFLECTIONS

Relax – Rely – Reflect.

> *Seek ye first the kingdom of God, . . . and all these things shall be added unto you.*
> *(Matthew 6:33)*

> *Be strong and of good courage, fear not, nor be afraid . . . for the Lord thy God, He it is that doth go with thee: He will not fail thee, nor forsake thee.*
> *(Deuteronomy 31:6)*

Quotation made famous by King George VI

'I said to the man who stood at the Gate of the Year, "Give me a light that I may tread safely into the unknown." And he replied, "Go out into the darkness, and put your hand into the hand of God. That shall be to you better than a light, and safer than a known way." '

It is important to realise that you are dealing with the most tremendous power in the world, when you pray.

Hope

Hope – what a wonderful word.

Hope, the Power of Suggestion is very strong in the human mind. Wonderful and powerful forces can be put into operation.

Hope is one of the basic principles in life, to continue when all seems lost.

One should never take anyone or anything for granted. Hope, this word brings a breath of fresh air, to blow away gloom, to awaken the heart and mind, that however low one has become, with perhaps tremendous burdens, there is Hope, that all will be well.

You should never let go of this word, which although a small word, can transform the whole outlook of existence.

Hope can transform a person, or situation. It can 'move mountains' in life. The mind changes, new energy flows through the mind and body when one has hope. The whole structure of life can be turned around, even disease can be halted. New thoughts, which can transform any situation, will be put into operation.

Never ever give up Hope. Hold on to it, it will change your life!

Silence

We often long for rest and release from the hammerings of this world. We dream of a lengthy stay in some paradise where nothing irks and nothing goes amiss. Failing this, the Isles of Greece or perhaps the Caribbean, might suffice for the renovation of jangled nerves and the disappointments of daily living. Few of us, however, can afford such therapies. We must go on with life as we find it.

Most of us are far too noisy in dealing with life. We talk compulsively about our ills and endlessly re-enact the wrongs we have endured. We tend to talk endlessly. We exhuast ourselves. Silence, though, is available. Its nourishing qualities have healing powers equal to the most idyllic haven of warmth and sunshine, and there is nothing to stop us apportioning a part of each day to a free excursion into it.

One should seek and find silence. It is a gift from God. Silence when one can be aware of the rustling of leaves. Silence can be a great healer. We have made so much noise in this world that silence is difficult to find.

Do try and find it; it will have a wonderful effect.

Peace of Mind

'Peace of Mind' is what almost all people throughout the world are trying to find, and have always sought, but few find it in its entirety. A little here and a little there seems to be the usual pattern. It is a most elusive state, but when found, it is heaven touching earth.

There are many reasons why it is not usually found. Mainly because people look for it in the wrong places. This often causes less peace of mind.

The only way to find true peace of mind is through God.

People tend to fluctuate, rather like a seesaw, up and down, up and down.

Even those with great faith can sometimes find it difficult in our present, turbulent world.

Having read this book, I hope that you will at least have received comfort and a real feeling of hope which may have eluded many of you in the past.

Perhaps you will have found one part of the book

particularly helpful. Re-read it, it may become more helpful than at first you realised.

There is no doubt that many people in our present generation have through faith and right living, changed their lives from hopelessness and deep despair to a full and astonishing 'new life'. One of happiness *and* peace of mind.

Whatever one does in this world, to make a real success of it one must work hard at it, and do one's best. The same applies to finding peace of mind. It does not usually 'drop from heaven, like the gentle rain'. It must be worked at.

'The Fundamental Issues' at the beginning of this book give a good guideline for one to follow. If at first you don't succeed, 'try, try and try again.' It is the people who have 'stickability' who usually win through. It may be hard perhaps to change your way of life and your thought process, but have a goal before you of a wonderful new existence. A mind free from worry, anxiety and hopelessness.

It is all there for anyone to gain, whatever position one may be in at present. It is up to oneself to start and continue in the right way, whatever temptations may come to lead one off the straight and narrow path. You will regret it. However tempting it may seem at the time.

If you do go astray, turn again, and get on the right track once more, find the elusive, heaven sent, peace of mind.

Future

What conclusions are we to draw from these 'Messages'?

There is definitely a God: a perfect God – Father-

Mother. One who loves *all* His children.

A God who has infinite resources to help His children in *this* sphere of existence and all existences.

That life for *all* is eternal. This life is a life for learning, before passing on to the next 'sphere of learning'.

That life IS spiritual. This is our *Real* Being. The Real Being is each of us eternally. We are separate spiritual beings, made in God, our Father's image and likeness – spiritually perfect. Like a drop in the ocean which has all the elements of the Great Ocean. As individuals we have lessons to learn to become eventually perfect, in eternity – like God's Son, who came down to earth to try to help us and to try to make us understand that God is our Father, and that life is eternal.

That we are *all* spiritual and children of the One Father, no matter what colour, race or religion we belong to. That there is *NO colour in Spirit.*

That our behaviour in this so-called material world is accountable for our next 'lives', in other spheres of existence.

That there is no Death, only a 'passing on'.

That love is the greatest quality for all peoples.

God has said, Christ has said, many times in the Bible it has said, 'Fear not. Fear is at the root of evil, and must be rooted out.

God has given us a wonderful world. We are His children. Let us not destroy our world, and let the people not destory themselves or others.

> *Hast thou not known? Hast thou not heard, that the everlasting God, the Lord, the Creator of the ends of the earth, fainteth not, neither is weary? There is no searching of his understanding. He giveth power to the faint; and to them that have no might he increaseth strength. Even the youths shall faint and be weary, and*

the young men shall utterly fall: but they that wait upon the Lord shall renew their strength; they shall mount up with wings as eagles; they shall run, and not be weary; and they shall walk, and not faint.
(Isaiah 40: 28-31)

I conclude by repeating the best piece of advice one can have. When in doubt:

Do what is nearest right in the circumstances and make sure your motives are right.

God bless you all.